YESTERDAY IN OREGON

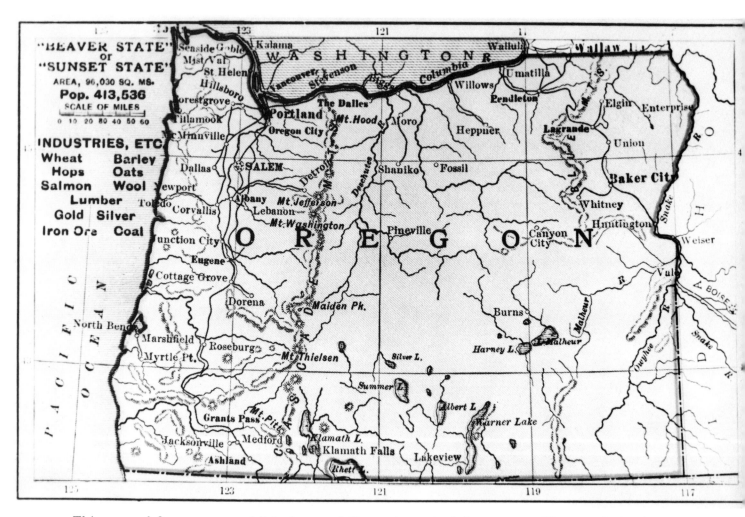

This map of Oregon was published around the early part of the century. The population in 1900 was 413,536. By 1980, the population for the state of Oregon had grown to 2,630,600.

YESTERDAY IN OREGON

A Pictorial Scrapbook

by

EDWIN D. CULP

The CAXTON PRINTERS, Ltd.
Caldwell, Idaho
1990

Library of Congress Cataloging-in-Publication Data

Culp, Edwin D.
    Yesterday in Oregon : a pictorial scrapbook / by
Edwin D. Culp.
        p.   cm.
    ISBN 0-87004-329-3 : $12.95
    1. Oregon--History--Pictorial works.   2. Oregon-
-Description and travel--Views.   I. Title.
F877.C84   1990
979.5--dc20   90-46636
                                                      CIP

Lithographed and bound in the United States of America by
The CAXTON PRINTERS, Ltd.,
Caldwell, Idaho
147751

TABLE OF CONTENTS

ACKNOWLEDGMENTS

I was very fortunate to be able to use the photographs of Ira Branch taken in Lincoln County in 1912. He was an amateur photographer but he turned out professional work.

Wanda Theobald Gifford loaned me the family collection of black and white photos taken at the turn of the century by her father-in-law, Benjamin Arthur Gifford, often called the dean of Oregon commercial photographers.

Various historical groups have been very helpful. Jean Shaw and Mildred Searcey of the Umatilla County Historical Society; Evelyn Hankes of the Clatsop County Historical Society; Addie Dyal of the Marion County Historical Society; Liz Winroth of the Oregon Historical Society; Lucy Skjelstad of the Horner Museum and Susan Niggli, Richard Crowe and Ralph Ewing of the Oregon State Library all gave of their time to helping with this publication.

Here are a few of the wonderful people who gave me a helping hand: Brooks Hawley of Baker County; Mrs. Lee Dickson of Redding, California; Dr. Wilmer Gardner of Oregon City; Mr. and Mrs. William May of The Dalles; Kathleen Richards of Cottage Grove; Kaye Richardson of Falls City; Eugene Stoller of Woodburn; Robert and Gladys Hunt along with Edgar A. Klippel of Corvallis; Allan Viewig, Bob Hoffman, Edwin C. Haack and George Skorney of Portland; Robert Lee Thompkins, Doris Martin, Minta Boyer and Ben Scruggs of Salem; and Lorraine Eckhardt of Cloverdale.

My family helped immensely as they have done on previous publications. My wife and daughter spent time making corrections while my son, a commercial photographer, handled the copy work.

I should never forget the helpfulness of the publisher and to thank Bobbi Humphries and Margaret Pead of Caxton's staff.

INTRODUCTION

I enjoy looking back. Most of my reading covers events taking place here in Oregon and is supplemented by all types of photographs, drawings, and newspapers. Recently I secured a copy of the June 1, 1859, issue of the *Sacramento Daily Union.* It was most revealing to find so much Oregon news in a daily California publication. Only three months before this date, Oregon had become the thirty-third state to be accepted into the Union.

Many of those prospecting for gold in California were former Oregonians and our political geographic happenings had a strong appeal to them. Communications between the West Coast and our cousins along the Atlantic seacoast were difficult, while ocean liners were sailing frequently between Oregon and California.

California was soon to have some changes in its transportation picture. These changes would affect the entire United States. In 1860, the Pony Express began a history-making operation by covering the two thousand mile trip from the Missouri River to California in an unheard of time of ten days.

Civil War clouds cast a shadow on Oregon's second year of statehood. The legislature, convened at Salem that year, faced the task of electing two United States senators. They found slavery and secession were fiery words among Oregonians. Many here felt Oregon was too remote from states in the east to become too involved. There was even a move to have California along with Oregon and the territory of Washington form a new republic entirely independent of our eastern states.

This same year, 1860, daily stage service between Portland and Sacramento was started. In the summertime, these coaches made a journey in seven days when the roads were dry and the weather good. When winter set in, the drivers and horses had to fight adverse weather conditions; it took twelve days and sometimes even more to make the trip.

In 1861, the Confederates fired on Fort Sumter and the Civil War was underway. The first Oregon State Fair was held the same year near Oregon City in Clackamas County emphasizing the importance of agriculture and the raising of livestock in this state. In 1862, the Oregon State Fair was moved to Salem in Marion County where it has remained to this day. Marion County with the state capital and the business it involved became the largest county in the state. The Homestead Act was passed by the U.S. Congress allowing settlers coming into Oregon to secure 160 acres of free land. This resulted in thousands of acres being opened up for settlement.

In 1862, the Oregon Portage Railroad was built from Bonneville to Cascade Locks, a distance of four and one-half miles. The portage line handled freight and passengers around this unnavigable part of the Columbia River. The Oregon Pony, the first steam locomotive in the Pacific Northwest, was used on this short line railroad. River transportation from the mouth of the Columbia River at Astoria to The Dalles was now open.

In 1863, another portage railroad was constructed with fourteen miles of trackage running between The Dalles and Celilo in

Wasco County, opening up another portion of the Oregon country. When the United States organized a territorial government in 1849, there were some eleven or twelve thousand inhabitants living for the most part west of the Cascade Mountains. Eastern Oregon and eastern Washington felt the effects of this new portage line as they were much closer to available markets.

In 1864, Oregon was linked with the rest of the country by the telegraph line. Today's news became the word. The next year brought the Civil War to an end. Alaska passed from Russian ownership into American hands. Portland was fast becoming the largest city in the Pacific Northwest.

In 1868, railroad construction was started in Portland towards California bringing our two states closer together. In 1869, the Central Pacific and the Union Pacific Railroads made a connection at a small point in Utah giving the country the first cross country rail service starting in the east and extending to California. It was not until 1883 that the second cross-country transcontinental line was completed by the Northern Pacific Railroad into Portland.

Transportation made and developed our Oregon country from the covered wagon that took three months to cross the continent to the present jet airlines that cover the same distance in hours. Oregon was moving into a new and much faster age. The former Oregon days were passing as a new era had arrived.

PROCEEDINGS

OF THE

Oregon State Agricultural Society,

AT THEIR

FIRST ANNUAL FAIR HELD IN CLACKAMAS COUNTY,

October 1st, 2d, 3d, and 4th, 1861,

INCLUDING THE LIST OF AWARDS, ADDRESSES, &C

— • —

PROCEEDINGS OF THE BOARD.

———

CLACKAMAS FAIR GROUNDS, Sept. 30, 1861.

The Board of Managers of the Oregon State Agricultural Society met this day. Present, J. Quinn Thornton, Albert G. Walling, J. S. Rinearson and Chester N. Terry.

G. Collier Robbins tendered his resignation as President of the Society.

On motion, the same was accepted.

LIST OF PREMIUMS

AWARDED BY THE

OREGON STATE AGRICULTURAL SOCIETY

AT ITS

SECOND ANNUAL FAIR,

HELD AT THE

Marion County Fair Grounds,

SEPTEMBER 30, AND OCTOBER 1, 2 & 3, 1862.

ALSO,

The Opening Address, by Maj. SIMEON FRANCIS, President of
the Society; Annual Address, by Hon. R. P. BOISE; and
Premium Essay, entitled "Oregon—its Resources,
Capabilities and Advantages, and the In-
ducements it offers to Immigrants."

————————•◆•————————

YESTERDAY IN OREGON

BAKER COUNTY

Main Street in Baker City looking north in 1913, with Court as the cross street. Notice the cupola on top of the building on the left side of the street. Neuberger & Heilner's Department Store, owned by Herman David, is on the right. Also on the right is the Geiser Grand Hotel, built in the 1880s as the Hotel Warshauer at a cost of $65,000. In the early 1900s it was purchased by the Albert Geiser family and renamed. The autos shown are all touring cars: a 1911 Overland *(left)*; a 1910 Packard *(center)* and a 1911 Pope Hartford *(right)*.

1889 Advertising

Mill Street in Sumpter. The bustling boom town was named after Fort Sumter, South Carolina by five Confederate soldiers who discovered gold near here in 1862. The buildings *(left to right)* are: Basche Hardware (sign shows only portion of name); the *Blue Mountain American,* a weekly newspaper started in 1896 with the name of *Sumpter News;* and the Bank of Sumpter, built in 1899 with A.P. Goss as its first president.

This early photo shows Sumpter Valley No. 2, a small wood-burning Brooks locomotive (2-6-0) built in 1881, pulling Caboose No. 02 through Boulder Gorge on Powder River, crossing Red Bridge enroute to Sumpter. This westbound train is some sixteen miles between Baker (in Baker County) and Prairie City (in Grant County).

The town of Copperfield in Baker County as it looked on July 4, 1900. The town existed for one purpose: to cater to the lack of inhibitions of the construction crews working and maintaining a nearby power plant and for railroad workers in surrounding areas. The town was referred to as "Gamorrah on the Snake (River)."

Whiskey was its lifeblood and vice was enjoyed undisturbed. There were no arrests, no peace officers, and no jail. In 1913, the Baker County sheriff reported that the town was impossible to handle. Governor Oswald West sent his secretary, Miss Fern Hobbs, a twenty-five-year-old, 105–pound gal, to Copperfield ordering those in charge of the town to resign their positions. She was accompanied by Lt. Col. B.K. Lawson and five soldiers of the Oregon National Guard. After failing to gain the town's support, she produced proclamation papers from her briefcase, prepared and signed by the governor, placing the town under martial law. The city officials were placed under arrest and "closed" signs were nailed on all gambling houses, saloons, and houses of ill repute. Miss Hobbs left on the evening train while the National Guard officers remained to make certain the closings were continued. Within one year the town shrank in population from one thousand to fifty, and was eventually destroyed by fire.

The *Portland Oregonian* covered the story of how Miss Fern Hobbs closed the town of Copperfield. "The crowd grew tense, when the council refused to resign. Miss Hobbs took a proclamation of martial law from her briefcase and called Col. Lawson forward to read it and place the council under arrest."

BENTON COUNTY

Dr. John Baptiste Horner and his family in 1889 enjoying the Corvallis countryside of their new Columbia bicycles. Dr. Horner was an educator, historian, and author; for forty-two years, he was on the staff of the Oregon Agriculture College, which today is Oregon State University. He is shown here with his wife, Isabelle Skipton Horner and their two daughters, Vera Delle Horner, age 12, and Pearl Alicia Horner (Wells), age 9.

Philomath College in Benton County was founded by the United Brethren Church and opened for classes in October of 1867 with about one hundred students. The college is located in Philomath, about six miles west of Corvallis. Classes taught here were designed to prepare students for theological seminary work, as many of the graduates became missionaries and ministers. The dormitory *(left)* was built in 1877 and the gym *(center)* was built in 1902-03. The brick building housing the college *(right)* is the oldest structure at the college and is still standing today. It was sold to the city of Philomath and leased to the Benton County Historical Society for a museum.

CIRCULAR
—OF—
Philomath College,
FOR 1870--71.
FACULTY:

Rev. T. J. CONNOR, - - - - **President.**
Prof. I. A. BIDDLE, (late of Oberlin Ohio), Principal and acting President.

We have ever since the establishment of our school, expected to secure the services of a competent Principal from the Atlantic States, but up to this time have been unsuccessful. We are now happy to inform our friends that we have secured the services of the above named Professor, and he comes to us highly recommended as a man well qualified to take charge of the school, and help make it a first class Institution.

This College is pleasantly situated in Philomath, Benton county, Oregon, six miles west of Corvallis. The location is a beautiful one, and surrounded with beautiful and romantic scenery, The College edifice is a substantial brick building two stories high, erected and finished in good style, at a cost of near twelve thousand dollars.

This College is now in its infancy having been first opened for the admission of students in November 1867. It is the intention of the Board of Trustees to afford the youth of Oregon the facilities for obtaining as thorough an education as at any of the colleges in the State. We know of no better place for families to reside and educate their children, as the community is composed of industrious farmers. We are free from grog shops with their contaminating influences to lead the youth estray.

Particular attention will be given to the moral training of pupils. The government of the school is mild, yet firm. The students will be expected to observe the regulations of the Institution.

Good boarding can be had in private families at $2 50 per week.

The College Year is divided into two sessions of five Calendar months each, the first beginning the first Tuesday in September and closing the first Saturday in February. The second beginning on the third Tuesday in February and closing on the third Saturday in July of each year.

TUITION:

Primary classes, per term of five months, - - - - $8 33
Advanced English classes, - - - - - - 12 50
Languages per term, (extra) - - - - - - 2 00
Incidental fee for Fall and Winter term, - - - - 1 00
" " " Spring and Summer Term, - - - 50

N. W. ALLEN, Agent.

Philomath, Benton County, Og'n., August 4th, 1870.

Gazette Print.

Fort Hoskins was built in Kings Valley by the U.S. Army to protect American settlers from Indians living on the Siletz reservation. This reservation area consisted of some one thousand square miles, which today would include most of Lincoln County along the Pacific Ocean and the cities of Newport, Toledo, and Waldport. Fort Hoskins was one of three forts constructed to encircle this group of Indians. This drawing shows how the fort looked when it was constructed. The long building *(top)* was the barracks and the mess hall was on the first floor. The officers' quarters were whitewashed and plastered *(below)* and occupied the three small buildings overlooking the valley. The hospital and guard house *(right)* were roughly three hundred feet east of the barracks. The buildings to the left housed the quartermaster, commissary, and laundries.

Hoskins in Benton County in 1960. This photo shows the headquarters of the Valley & Siletz Railroad (V&S) with V&S No. 7, an Elco seventy-ton diesel-electric locomotive *(center)*, which was purchased new in 1954. C. Lee and Mary O'Kelly's General Store and railroad station is to the right and a corner of a white covered bridge, which crosses the Upper Luckiamute River, can be seen to the extreme right. Today this entire area is a ghost town, as the tracks and buildings are gone.

A 1910 crowd waits in front of the Corvallis railroad station for the daily train to Newport to enjoy the cool ocean breeze.

CLACKAMAS COUNTY

An O&C railroad ticket from Oregon City to Clackamas—a distance of four miles.

The first issue of the *Oregon Spectator* was published in Oregon City in 1846. It was the first newspaper issued west of the Rockies.

The Oregon Statesman.

The *Oregon Statesman* was first issued in Oregon City, the territorial capital, on March 28, 1851. It is the second oldest newspaper in the Northwest. The first *Statesman* was printed at Oregon City on a hand-operated press which came around the Horn from Massachusetts. The Statesman followed the territorial capital to Salem in 1853, then to Corvallis in 1855, then finally back to Salem for permanent residence a few months later.

Charles David Latourette, lawyer and former mayor of Oregon City, sitting in the front seat of a 1911 Packard touring car. The car is parked in front of the New Era General Merchandise store and post office where Mrs. J.N. Dustin was postmaster and manager of the store.

The city of Clackamas in 1920, looking down Clackamas Avenue. The city of Clackamas was originally called Marshfield, but upon applying for a post office in 1870 had to choose another name as there was already a Marshfield in Coos County. The name was then changed to Clackamas with some thought given to the former Clackamas City, which had been located about two miles away on the south bank of the Clackamas River, and about a half-mile upriver from the confluence with the Willamette River. This town was completely washed away in the flood of 1861. The General Merchandise Store (left) was built by Arthur Mather in 1870, one year after the railroad entered the area. The Oregon & California Railroad published its first operating timetable in 1870, and showed the town as Marshville, apparently in error. Mather's store was built on the level with the railroad tracks, but after Southern Pacific secured ownership of the tracks in 1887, the track was lowered eight feet to eliminate the roller coaster effects of its main line right-of-way. Mather had to add steps to his store, and build a rock wall along the front. The many cars along the edge of the road belong to people visiting Camp Withycombe (left, but not pictured). The camp belonged to the state of Oregon and was used as a rifle range and national guard encampment. Note the safety bell above the railroad "cross-buck," a warning signal later replaced by the "wig-wag" system of today.

The local confectionery store in the small community of Milwaukie was located on Front Street, now McLaughlin Boulevard. This store served as a ticket office and waiting area for interurban patrons using the traction service of the Portland Railway Light & Power Company cars to Portland or Oregon City. Waiting for the train are *(left to right)*: Bob Ganyard; M.O. Hadden; Will Kelso (owner of the store); Ellen and Bess Roberts; and Judge John Kelso.

Gladstone is a small community located about ten miles south of Portland and borders on the Clackamas River. This 1912 photo shows the Portland Light and Power Company railroad station located between the Richard Freytag Grocery Store and H.W. Strebig's Meat Market. The man in the apron is Mr. Strebig. Notice the railroad tracks down the middle of Arlington Street. The cross street is Portland Boulevard.

Carver Park in the summer of 1930, located along the cool and delightful Clackamas River. The Clackamas & Eastern Railway bridge *(left)* is under construction. A partially constructed railroad bridge built by Stephen Carver before World War I was torn down to make way for this structure. Baker's Bridge *(right)* was a covered highway bridge which was dismantled in the 1930s so that a new steel truss bridge could be built. Automobiles shown are of a 1925-26 vintage.

In 1904, the interurban railroad running from Portland to Oregon City extended its trackage about a mile and a half in order to serve the small community of Canemah located above the Falls at Oregon City. At the same time they purchased the old run-down Canemah Park, a flat acreage located on top of a hill overlooking the town. Picnic tables were installed, along with stoves, a baseball diamond and a dancing pavilion. The park became a favorite attraction for families in Portland. They would board the large, electrified open-air cars at Second and Alder Streets for the fourteen-mile trip to the entrance of the park. To make the trip even more enjoyable, the traction company offered a special inducement of using the cars in one direction while the return trip could be made on riverboats. It was a Sunday outing that had real charm and only cost twenty-five cents for the round trip fare. Families would arrive with their picnic baskets and every member of the family found something to his or her enjoyment.

The arrival of the interurban open-air railroad at Canemah Park, with the Willamette River in the background.

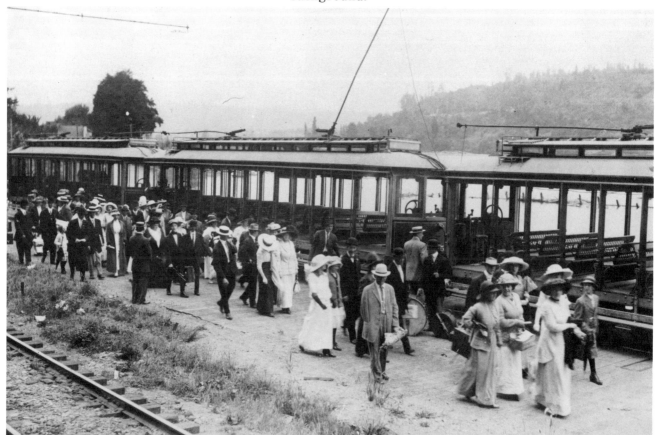

The pavilion at Canemah Park was a favorite for dancing.

A band was on hand every Sunday at Canemah Park.

A group of "Happy Hour" enthusiasts at Lake Oswego, presumably during the days of Prohibition, as reference to "near beer" and "soft drinks" is made. Many inquiries for additional information on this photo, which is a print made from a glass negative, were made, but to no avail. Can you help?

CLATSOP COUNTY

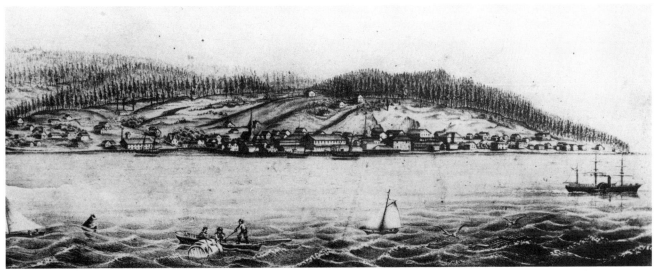

Astoria in Clatsop County was the first American settlement on the Pacific Coast. It is one of the most historic spots in America, bearing to the Pacific Coast much the same relation that Plymouth does to the Atlantic Coast. Oregon's oldest city was first settled on May 11, 1811, by trappers, clerks, and fur traders of John Jacob Astor's Pacific Fur Company. The site selected was an elevated point of land jutting into the Columbia River between two shallow bays. Here, Fort Astoria was constructed. This drawing shows Astoria as it looked in 1870.

Astoria as photographed from the same spot one hundred years later in 1970.

DAILY TOVERI'S BULLETIN

City Destroyed by Flames

Damage Estimated at Thirty Million. --- Fire Under Control

The business district of Astoria burned up this morning. All of forty blocks of the business section of the city have been consumed by the conflagration.

The fire started about 2 o'clock this morning in the basement of Thiel's pool hall, which was near the Bee Hive department store, on Twelfth and Commercial streets. It is not known as yet how the fire originated. The fire spread under the streets, which in this section of the city were built on pilings. The fire broke up above the surface in three or four different parts of the city. When once above the surface the fire spread rapidly in the face of a strong wind. The wooden buildings caught fire quickly and flamed up like tinder, spreading the fire from block to block in a few moments.

The city is now a smouldering heap of ruins from Exchange Street to the waterfront and from Seventh Street to Seventeenth Street. In this area all the buildings were burned except the Spexarth Building, Sixth and Commercial Sts., and the Lower Columbia Creamery plant, Ninth and Duane Sts., which being fireproof buildings were not totally destroyed.

The devastated area contained over fifty large buildings such as hotels, large department stores, restaurants, office buildings, etc. which are completely burned to the ground. The city's four banks are a heap of ashes. About fourty garages, filled with new and used automobiles were consumed by the angry flames.

The total damage done by the conflagration will amount to over 30 million dollars.

The city fire department could not check the flames as they quickly spread from building to building. A call for help was sent to Portland. A fire boat from Portland arrived at four o'clock. More fire apparatus arrived from Portland on the 5:15 train. Three fire-trucks also arrived in good time from Portland. By the joint efforts of the two fire departments the conflagration has now been checked.

Several persons killed

It is impossible to say at this time how many persons have been killed in the fire, as reports concerning the fatalities are conflicting and unreliable. Among the dead are reported to be Mr. Norris Staples, president of the Bank of Commerce, who died from heart failure, a sailor from the Bark Oneonta was drowned at the O. W. R. & N. docks as the roof of a burning building fell on him.

Relief is provided

Relief headquarters have been opened at the Y. M. C. A. building. The Seaside Hotel at Seaside has been opened and is offering shelter for those who lost their homes. A free bus leaves the Y. building and all those wishing to go to Seaside are requested to call at the Y.

Mayor Bremner has called a general mass meeting of the business men and the city officials, to meet at the City Hall at two o'clock this afternoon. Relief measures will be discussed.

DECISIONS OF MASS MEETING.

Nobody allowed on burned area. Hundred men assigned on guard duty.

All business men will meet tomorrow morning at nine o'clock at the City Hall.

Fire swept through the business district of Astoria on December 8, 1922, leaving 2500 people homeless and causing several thousand dollars worth of property damage. The *Morning Astorian* was destroyed by fire but the employees worked forty-four hours without sleep to put the paper back into operation within four days. Here, the Astoria Finnish newspaper, *The Toveri*, published the first account of the fire.

ASTORIA'S GREAT CENTENNIAL CELEBRATION AUGUST 10th to SEPTEMBER 9th.

Morning Astorian.

THE NEW WAY.
for better and trade is through the Classified Columns of the Morning Astorian. Be modern and get results.

WEATHER
Oregon and Washington fair today.

38th YEAR.   NO. 206   ASTORIA, OREGON, TUESDAY, AUGUST 29, 1911.   FIVE CENTS

SCANDINAVIANS TODAY CELEBRATE FOUNDING OF OREGON

SERENADE MRS. HARE, CENTENARIAN

GREAT STREET PARADE IN AFTERNOON

ASTOR PRAISED IN SPECIAL PROGRAM

MAYOR READS MESSAGE FROM DESCENDENT OF PACIFIC COAST PIONEER FUR TRADER.

B. F. CRAWSHAW MAKES TALK

CROWDS CHEER PATRIOTIC ADDRESSES IN STADIUM.

30,000 ASTER BLOSSOMS GIVEN AWAY TO VISITORS

Throngs Gather at Home of Frances Ellen Hare When Ellery's Royal Italian Band Plays Stirring Music; Centennial Officials and Others Address and Pay Homage to Woman Who Was Born Three Months Before the Landing of Astor's Party on the Oregon Shores.

Commercial street and up Nieth to the centenarian's home. Filling into the yard the band gathered in front of the window and played several stirring selections. Dr. Henderson addressed the gathering and after paying tribute to the noted Astorian handed her a handsome bouquet of Asters. Manager Tremp presented her with an Astoria Centennial pennant.

At the request of Mrs. Hare, Miss Sweeney, singer at the Weinhard-Astoria grill, rendered "Nearer My God to Thee," accompanied by a clarionettist from Ellery's band, and invited the members of the band and the public to shake hands with her. Mrs. Hoagland and Mrs. Gilman presented
(Continued on Page Five.)

○○○○○○○○○○○○○○○○
○ TRYING TO BUY OFF   ○
○   ARRESTING POLICE.   ○
○   ○
○ There have been numerous in- ○
○ stances reported at Headquarters ○
○ during the past few days of men, ○
○ arrested for vagrancy, offering ○
○ pieces of money to the arresting ○
○ policemen to "square" the trans- ○
○ action before being taken to   ○
○ Headquarters.   ○
○ All such propositions have   ○
○ been turned down, he it said to ○
○ the credit of the men of the de- ○
○ partment.   ○
○ It has been unofficially sug-   ○
○ gested that when such affairs are ○
○ placed within judicial informa- ○
○ tion of the Court, the penalty   ○
○ prescribed should be "8"sted" in ○
○ due proportion.   ○
○○○○○○○○○○○○○○○○

Total Abstainers in Session.

Today's Official Centennial Program

TUESDAY, AUGUST 29.— SCANDINAVIAN DAY.

Forenoon.
Reception of guests and visitors.

Afternoon.
2:00 P. M.—Formation of parade.
2:30 P. M—Spectacular Scandinavian parade and pageant.
3:30 P. M.—Exercises in Stadium. Program as follows:—

1. Overture by Ellery's Band.
2. Invocation by Rev. Richard Olson.
3. Introductory remarks by L. O. Belland, Pres. Scandinavian Day.
4. Address of Welcome. Dr. H. L. Henderson, Mayor.
5. Response. Hans Bugge, Pres. Sons of Norway.
6. Vocal Solo, Miss Rose Robinson, of Portland.
7. Address, Governor West.
8. Violin Selection, Miss Esther Sundquist, Pianist, Miss Anna Larsen.
9. Address, Rev. Bergersen, of Ballard, Wash.
10. Vocal Solo, Miss Rose Robinson.
11. Violin Selection, Miss Esther Sundquist.
12. Address, Prof. David Nyvall, of Seattle, Wash.
"America" by Audience.

Night.
8:00 P. M.—Concert by Ellery's Band, Indian War Dances at Stadium.
Ellery Band Program.

1. March, El Capitan, Sousa.
2. Poet and Peasant, Suppe.
3. Cornet Solo, "My Heart and Thy Sweet Voice," Saint Saens, Mr. D'Amico.
4. Grand Duet from Norma, Bellini, for two trumpets, Messrs. D'Amico and Grassi.

Part II.

5. Chocolate Soldier, Strauss.
6. Naila, Pas De Fleurs, De Siles.
7. Vocal Solo, Selected, Mr. Wallace.
8. Grand Selection Il Trovatore, Verdi. Anvil Chorus—Miserere—Solos by

W. U. MAN MARRIES

Takes Brooklyn Girl for Bride in East Today.

William J. Smith, district superintendent for the Western Union Telegraph company, who was an early Centennial visitor in the city, will today claim as his bride, Miss Teresa Trayer, of 389 Clinton street, Brooklyn, New York.

Soon after leaving Astoria when he attended the Centennial opening, Mr. Smith left for New York and Brooklyn. The couple will spend a short time in the East and then will return to the coast, visiting Astoria before settling down in their permanent home in Seattle.

Rich Prizes for Crack Shots
SPIRIT LAKE, Aug. 28:—Several score of the most prominent trap shooters of the country rounded up today at Orleans, on the south shore of Spirit Lake, to compete in the annual national tournament of the "Indians." The programme and entry list combine to give promise of one of the best tournaments of the year. The contests will last four days and prizes amounting to more than $1,000 a day will be distributed among the winning marksmen.

SWIMMERS TO COMPETE

MULTNOMAH AND PORTLAND Y. M. C. A. ARE FAVORED.

Program Includes One Mile Championship, Fancy Swimming and

GREAT STREET PARADE IN AFTERNOON

DESCENDENTS OF FORMER RESIDENTS OF THREE COUNTRIES UNITE IN MONSTER PAGEANT.

PREPARE A FINE PROGRAM

350 SCANDINAVIAN-AMERICANS ARRIVED YESTERDAY.

TRAINS AND STEAMERS BRING BIG CROWDS.

Parade Will Include Nine Big New Floats Prepared Especially for the Occasion, Grand Lodge Scandinavian Brotherhood of America Comes Here For Holiday Before Meeting in Portland.

○○○○○○○○○○○○○○○
○   ○
○ Mayor H. L. Henderson last ○
○ night stated that he hoped, so ○
○ far as possible, all the stores, in ○
○ whatever line of trade, would   ○
○ accept the appropriateness of   ○
○ closing their doors this afternoon. ○
○ Such general closing movement   ○
○○○○○○○○○○○○○○○

The Daily Independent.

VOL. I.   ASTORIA, OREGON: TUESDAY, MARCH 18, 1884.   No. 39

CURRENT FARM TOPICS.

Valuable Information for the Farmer and Dairyman.

Short Hints that will Prove Beneficial to the Readers of the Independent, Gathered from the Most Reliable Sources.

A Massachusetts farmer drove his horse—which is in excellent condition—for a load of wood. When ready to return he showed himself an aggravating balker; he declined to pull a pound. Instead of trying to persuade him with a club the owner tied the refractory animal to a tree and let him stand. At sunset he was again vainly invited to move. The rest of the story we quote from the Fitchburg Sentinel: "I made up my mind that when that horse went to the barn he would take that load of wood. The night was not cold. I covered him warm, and he stood until morning. He drew that load of wood the first time I asked him. I returned and got another load before I fed him. I then rewarded him with a good dinner. I have drawn several loads since. Once he refused to draw, but soon as he saw me start for the house he started after me with the load at once.

Here are a few useful items from the Rural New Yorker: "Who hears of the President Garfield tomato now? And what a splurge is made in 1882.—There are many grand varieties of the clematis, but if we could have but one it would be Jackmanii.—Hereafter I shall plant radishes in the warmest, most sheltered spot that I can find, make the soil very rich and surround the bed with a frame.—Why not have a climbing rose? Would it not improve the barn, wash house, smoke house, piazza? Most of the varieties are perfectly hardy. They bloom in profusion for a long time. Prairie Queen (pink), Bennett's seedling (white) and Russell's cottage (crimson) would make a good selection. It should be borne in mind that these roses bloom on the old or last season's wood."

Mr. E. Williams mentions in the Chatham Courier the clearest and simplest

ment will follow. He once raised a fine brood in early spring by keeping their coop on wheels, and changing it so as to keep them in the sun much of the time."

A Minnesota correspondent of the Western Rural pleads for justice to the common cow, amid the current praises of thoroughbreds, and a fair chance of improvement: "Had we better leave our native out in the cold, without any good word as to her being an all-purpose cow? It will not be denied that the native will stand more abuse and give better returns than any known breed. Does it not stand to reason they can be bred up and cared for in such a way that they may in time become superior, take as any other for general purposes? I think they can; it is a fact that there has been but little pains taken to improve the natives as natives, and yet you will find native cows that will make from twelve to sixteen pounds of butter per week for four months without extra feed, and hold out as long as any. Are they not better for the average western farmer than the high-priced extra-blooded animals? High-priced stock calls for better stables and more grain."

Mrs. Field writes to the Prairie Farmer that if the system of corn improvement long practiced by an agriculturist of her acquaintance were generally adopted there would be less loss of crop by early frost, and a certainty of good seed. "When he went to farming forty years ago he bought a peck of seed corn of the northern yellow flint variety, and as he 'don't believe in running after all the new seeds that are advertised' he is still raising the same variety—only it ripens some three weeks earlier than it did then. Every fall he goes through his field and selects seed from the best of the earliest ripening; when these are husked one or two lusks are left on each, and then braided together until there are fifteen or twenty ears in a string. These strings are hung up in the sun for a fortnight or so, and then hung from the rafters in a cool, dry loft over the woodshed; there it remains till seed time, and it never fails to grow."

French Prepared for War.
France learned a lesson from the last

Astoria in May, 1905, with the Vice President of the United States, Charles Warren Fairbanks, standing in the rear of a 1905 Maxwell touring car. He will be President Theodore Roosevelt's representative at the Lewis & Clark Centennial Exposition and Oriental Fair in Portland on June 1, the opening day. The Astoria & Columbia River railroad station is in the center of the picture.

COLUMBIA COUNTY

Keasey is a logging community on Rock Creek forty miles northwest of St. Helens in Columbia County and was built and developed after World War I. It is served by The Portland, Astoria & Pacific Railway running between Vernonia and Keasey for a connection here with several logging lines reaching deep into the timber areas. The East Side Lumber Company is one of these lines, and pictured here are its living quarters *(right)* and one of its shay-type locomotives, a Willamette gear engine No. 102, along with the railroad station *(far rear)*.

The stern-wheeler riverboat *Shaver* in 1910 towing a one-thousand-foot log raft down the Columbia River to Astoria. From there an ocean-going tug will handle these logs for the next eleven hundred miles to San Diego, California—a trip that will last some fourteen or fifteen days. During the summer months, Simon Benson, a resourceful lumber king at the time, would ship millions of board feet of Douglas fir lumber to California after binding these logs together into large cigar-shaped rafts tied with heavy chains. It was far cheaper to take the logs over water than to pay the freight charges offered by the railroad.

One of Simon Benson's log rafts in the middle of the Columbia River headed toward the Pacific Ocean with the town of Stella, Washington, in the background. The vessels are *(left to right)*: the stern-wheeler *Lurline*; steam tug *Tatoosh*; steam schooner *Arctic*; and the stern-wheeler *Charles R. Spencer*.

COOS COUNTY

SOUTHERN PACIFIC LINES

Coos Bay Line
TIME TABLE

Subject to change without notice

F. S. McGINNIS,
Passenger Traffic Manager

JOHN M. SCOTT,
Asst. Passenger Traffic
Manager
Portland, Oregon

In 1906 Southern Pacific purchased this short twenty-six-mile rail line and extended the trackage for a connection with its own railroad in Eugene, opening up a previously isolated territory. The city of Coos Bay is in the background. Notice the coal chute *(right)*. Here, carloads of coal are shoved up the steep incline into the bunker for use by ocean-going vessels.

CROOK COUNTY

Prineville is the county seat of Crook County. The two leading industries in the area are lumber and livestock. The Hotel Prineville, located at Third and Main streets, was built in 1907 and destroyed by fire in 1922. It was owned and operated by Charles E. McDowell. The auto is a 1908 Premier.

This log cabin near Prineville was built at the turn of the century by homesteaders who came by covered wagon to settle in Central Oregon. The home has two rooms with a loft above and a wood shed attached on the rear. Notice the "stick and mud" fireplace with a metal protector to keep it upright. The roof is of white pine shakes, split by a frow-cleaving tool. A large tree in front offers some shade while a springhouse *(right)* supplies drinking water.

CURRY COUNTY

A small group of pioneers established a settlement in Port Orford in 1851. They had been attacked by Indians and taken refuge here on Battle Rock, a nearby location. Bitter deprivation and desperate fighting followed. The small group escaped and made their way to a settlement on the Umpqua River. Today the city of Port Orford is located on a beautiful deep-water bay along the Pacific Ocean, and has the dubious honor of being the western-most city on the mainland United States.

The Port Orford Tribune.

olume XIII. PORT ORFORD, OREGON, WEDNESDAY, AUGUST 10, 1904. Number 17

OFFICIAL DIRECTORY.

STATE AND DISTRICT OFFICERS:

Sen—John H. Mitchell of Portland and Chas. Fulton of Astoria
...ressman, First District—Binger Hermann, of Roseburg.
...rnor—Geo. E. Chamberlain Salem.
...tary of State—F. I. Dunbar, Salem.
Treasurer—Chas. S. Moore, Salem.
Public Instruction—J. H. Ackerman, Salem.
Printer—J. R. Whitney, Salem.
...ey General—A. M. Crawford, Salem.
State Land Board—G. G. Brown, Salem.
Senator for Coos and Curry—...hn S. Coke.
Representative for Coos and Curry—Robert Burns.
..., 2d Judicial District—J. W. Hamilton, Roseburg.
...uting Attorney, 2d Judicial District—George M. Brown, Roseburg.
...Commissioners—J. H. Upton, ...glois.

COUNTY OFFICERS.

...ty Judge—E. A. Bailey, Gold Beach.
...ty Commissioners—J. W. Cooley, ...hetco; C. W. Haines, Eckley.
...ff—S. E. Marsters, Gold Beach.
...ty Clerk—George W. Smith, Gold Beach.
...ty Treasurer—James Caughell, Wedderburn.
...sor—A. J. Marsh, Port Orford.
...l Supt.—Ames S. Johnston, Port Orford.
...eyor—R. J. Canfield Agness.
...ner—Dr. T. C. Green, Port Orford.

MEETINGS OF THE COURTS.

...it Court meets Fourth Monday in August of each year.
...ty Commissioners Court meets first Wednesday in January, April, July and September of each year.
...ate Court meets first Monday in each month.

...Y COUNTY POST OFFICES AND POST-

HALL'S VEGETABLE SICILIAN Hair Renewer

Is it true you want to look old? Then keep your gray hair. If not, then use Hall's Hair Renewer, and have all the dark, rich color of early life restored to your hair.

P. J. MASTERSON,

PORT ORFORD, OREGON,

DEALER IN

GENERAL MERCHANDISE

KEEPS IN STOCK,

GROCERIES, The Best, Only,

DRY GOODS.

TIMBER LAND, ACT JUNE 3, 1878.—NOTICE FOR PUBLICATION.

United States Land Office, Roseburg, Oregon, July 27, 1904. Notice is hereby given that in compliance with the provisions of the act of Congress of June 3, 1878, entitled "An act for the sale of timber lands in the States of California, Oregon, Nevada, and in Washington Territory," as extended to all the Public Land States by act of August 4, 1892, Mrs. Ida H. Iles, of Everett, county of Snohomish, State of Washington, has this day filed in this office her sworn statement No. 6332, for the purchase of the Lots 1, 2, and 3, in section No. 7, Township 33 S., R. 14 W., and will offer proof to show that the land sought is more valuable for its timber or stone than for agricultural purposes, and to establish her claim to said land before the Register and Receiver of this office at Roseburg, Oregon, on Thursday, the 20th day of October, 1904.

He names as witnesses: L. L. Iles, David Iles, George Wents, Charles Wise, all of Everett, Washington.

Any and all persons claiming adversely the above-described lands are requested to file their claims in this office on or before said 20th day of October, 1904.

J. T. BRIDGES, Register.

TIMBER LAND, ACT JUNE 3, 1878.—NOTICE FOR PUBLICATION.

United States Land office, Roseburg, Oregon, May 24, 1904. Notice is hereby given that in compliance with the provisions of the act of Congress of June 3, 1878, entitled "An act for the sale of timber lands in the States of California, Oregon, Nevada, and Washington Territory," as extended to all the Public Land States by act of August 4, 1892, Fred. T. Sanderson, of Bandon, County of Coos, State of Oregon, has this day filed in this office his sworn statement No. 6173, for the purchase of the $E\frac{1}{2}$ $NW\frac{1}{4}$, $NE\frac{1}{4}$ $SW\frac{1}{4}$ section 31, in Township No. 32 south, range No. 14 west, and will offer proof to show that the land sought is more valuable for its timber or stone than for agricultural purposes, and to establish his claim to said land before Charles T. Blumenbrother, U. S. Commissioner, at his office at Bandon, Coos county, Oregon, on Saturday, the 20th day of August, 1904.

He names as witnesses: T. Allen, Winter D. Davison, both of Bandon, Oregon, William R. Hurst, of Port Orford, Oregon, William Hurst,

WHEN THE FUSE BLOWS.

No Occasion for Alarm—In Fact It Proves Motor's Safety—The Device Explained.

The "blowing" of a fuse in an electric street car, which fills the average passenger with alarm, simply indicates that a safety device has proved reliable and that a danger of injury to the motor has been averted by it, says the New York Herald. The current which will flow through a motor when it is standing still is in almost all cases far in excess of that which the motor is designed to carry; and, indeed, in a well designed motor a current dangerous for the motor will be reached before the motor has been stalled. The effect of this heavy current on the motor, if allowed to continue, is to heat the windings to a dangerous degree and destroy the insulation, possibly setting it on fire; and it is to prevent this occurrence, whether due to careless handling of the car or to unexpected causes, that the fuses are used. A fuse is simply a short piece of wire of such size that it will be melted by a current which, if allowed to flow through the motor for any time, will damage it. The melting of the fuse opens the circuit and cuts off the current from the motor. To protect the car the fuse is inclosed in a fireproof box.

When the fuse blows there is generally a volatilization of the metal of the fuse and a slight explosion. These explosions usually cause a report and some smoke.

Two Centuries Ago.

The earliest instance known of penalizing smoking in the streets is in the court books of the mayor of Methwold in England. There is the following entry on the record of the court held October 14, 1695: "We agree that any person that is taken smoaking tobacco in the street shall forfitt one shillinge for every time so taken, and it shall be lawful for the petty constables to distraine for the same, for to be put to the uses above said. We present Nicholas Barber for smoaking in the street, and doo amerce him one shillinge."

Earliest Map of Oregon.

A map of Oregon published in 1859 by S. J. McCormick, of Portland, probably the first large wall map of the state ever printed, has been placed in possession of the Oregon Historical society by

ORIGIN OF BASKET BALL.

First Played at Training School in Springfield, Mass., in the Year 1891.

Basket ball as a recreative game is unique in its origin for two reasons. Firstly, it is our one, positively sure, home American production; secondly, the name, date and place of its authorship are exactly known, says Golden Days. Of no other game in all the category can this be said; the birth of the bulk of them is buried in an obscurity which reaches beyond the cuneiform-covered, baked clay tablets of Babylon, and the hieroglyphics of the remotest Egyptian records.

Basket ball, on the other hand, was born in the year 1891 at Springfield, Mass., and its author was James Naismith.

In that town is a training school connected with the Young Men's Christian Association, and, of course, professors, among them a professor of psychology, who is paid to teach the young ideas how to think, effectively. In one of his lectures he called attention to certain conditions upon which the brain could with advantage be exercised, and challenged his class to supply the requirements to meet them. The conditions were the invention of a new game which could be played indoors, in a limited area, by a defined and unalterable number of contestants, and adaptable to both sexes.

Upon this hypothesis one of his pupils, James Naismith, the same night evolved "basket ball." It was put into practice the next day, experimentally, and found to meet the conditions and limitations laid down by the professor admirably. But it had more than an academic value, as its rapid spread as one of the most appreciated

THE MAKING OF LENSES.

Glass Is Made Principally in European Countries and Shipped in Small Slabs.

When a popular camera was first under consideration, it became necessary to secure a good lens at a popular price. This was possible only by the devising and making of special machinery and tools, and by buying the raw glass and manufacturing in large quantities, writes W. B. Ashley, in Outing. Lens glass, as all the world knows, or will after this story is published, is made principally in Germany, France and England. Brought to the manufacturer in small slabs, it is cut by revolving saws into the different sizes and then subjected to a series of grindings and polishings that must eventually enable the tester to find the lens over an absolute form of the shape and size required, so perfectly that a deviation of one two millionth of an inch is instantly detected. The cement used for building up lenses from single lenses is a preparation so delicate that it cannot alter this perfection. The making of lenses for photographic work has now become an immense industry, and in many cases the shutters are also made in conjunction. Highest skill is employed to perfect this first requisite of the apparatus, but careful as these makers are to prove their work, the lenses are also always thoroughly tested by the camera experts. This does not mean that they are subjected to anything like the different tests the amateur will apply later on, but finish, focus and mount, and the focal scale is tested by objects at the stated distances; the finder is brought into alignment, and then the camera needs only the final touching up of rubbed spots to be ready for the market.

PORT ORFORD POST.

VOL. II. PORT ORFORD, OREGON: THURSDAY, JUNE 30, 1881. NO. 5.

THE POST.

J. H. UPTON & SON, Proprietors.

Published Every Thursday,

...AT...

PORT ORFORD, CURRY CO., OR.

SUBSCRIPTION RATES.

One Year	$2.00
Six Months	1.25
Three Months	.75

ADVERTISING RATES REASONABLE.

L. P. FISHER, Advertising Agent, 21 Merchant's Exchange, San Francisco, is authorized to receive advertisements for the columns of this paper.

Discontinued Operations—Bitten by a Sea Lion.

Messrs. Chas. Brown and Dennis Cahniff came in from the rocks yesterday afternoon, having discontinued sealing operations for the season. They would not have withdrawn so early had not Dennis met with a mishap which in a meas-

Mrs. Rachel Knapp.

Seeing it stated in a Baker City paper as an interesting fact that a lady in that town weighs 225 pounds, it occurs to us to mention the fact that in Port Orford resides a lady—Mrs. Rachel Knapp—who weighs upward of that figure, and yet she is not deemed a prodigy of averdupois. Mrs. Knapp is 78 years of age, and is in the enjoyment of good health and of a mind and memory unclouded by the weight of the multiplied decades which have come and gone since she stepped upon the stage of active existence. She walks briskly, experiencing little more than ordinary fatigue, considerable distances visiting among neighbors and friends. With her own hands, she cultivates year after year, probably the best garden in the county, digs and garners her crop of potatoes, and exercises a general and lively superintendence over the affairs of the household, which in-

Wool.

Shearing in this county is well advanced, and the clip will be above the average; while no sales to speak of have been made hereabouts of the new clip. Generally the buyers have been in the field heretofore earlier than this, bidding for this staple. It is not too late yet, however; the sheep men will hold on. A fair offer will be had ere long. The latest we have on the subject from the valley is that 25 cents was being paid at Roseburg. Curry county wool rates up with the highest Oregon.

Assistant Clerk.

Mr. A. M. Gillespie occupied the desk as assistant Clerk during Court week for Walter Sutton. He did the office work while the Clerk was engaged in attendance upon the Circuit Court.

The Races.

All entries must be closed on or before the third, in the Ellens-

Prof. Allen—"Conundrum" Examinations.

We notice in Prof. Powell's announcement of the forthcoming Teachers' Association, that Prof. Chas. H. Allen, of the Normal School, San Jose, will be present. We should be sorry to see some of the notions and theories of Prof. Allen engrafted upon the Common School system of this State; and especially would we dislike to see our State Board of Examination adopt his method of "conundrum" examinations—a method eminently adapted to the ascertainment of what the applicant does not know, and that which, for any practical end, it were folly for him to know. Prof. Allen is responsible for the inauguration of this pedantic, supercilious method in California. Then followed a harvest—a very saturnalia of corruption and debauchery in educational circles in most of the more populous sections of that State. Veteran teachers were confronted with the alternative of taking a course in the "Normal School" or abdicating a profession to which they were devotedly attached, and in the duties of which some of them had spent half a life time, or of taking back

pers, of whom Prof. Allen was thought to be the chief, inaugurate a reign of spoliation, and injustice, and nonsense, the results of which when developed, shocked the moral sense of the Golden State from center to its utmost confines. Oregon wants none of it.

From Rogue River.

A Rogue river correspondent sends the following:

The crops are looking well on the river, but I don't know how long they will be so, for the grasshoppers are as thick as graybacks on a bummer's corpus. They are taking the grass as clean as they can.

There is no one logging on the river now except Mr. Huntley, who is logging on a small scale.

Mr. W. R. Miller got a bad cut on his arm a few days ago, but is now doing well.

The pack train that passed through Port Orford was packing the family of Mr. King to Rogue river to reside. They are not satisfied with this country, but I guess they will have to stay, for they are like the rest of us—they can't get away. The widow that was with them is living with Mr.

DESCHUTES COUNTY

Main Street in Bend, 1919. Note the unpaved streets. The auto in the middle of the road is a 1913 Overland. The first car parked diagonally *(extreme right)* is a 1918 Chevrolet. Others are various models built by Henry Ford.

The Dalles-California Highway, ten miles south of Bend, in 1919 before U.S. Highway 97 was built. This area is a mass of lava volcanic cones from Lava Butte. A Model T Ford moves cautiously over the rough terrain.

Redmond is in Deschutes County but before 1916 was in Crook County. Here is Redmond in 1912 looking down Sixth Street, which was paved in 1935. Notice the 1909 Buick *(right)*, believed to be the first car in Redmond. It was owned by Frank McCaffery. The buildings on the left side of the street *(left to right)* are: Hotel Redmond with F.W. White, owner (this hotel was destroyed by fire in 1927); Gregory's Variety Store; the State Bank of Redmond with G.H. Ehler, cashier; Redmond Grill; the *Oregon Hub*, a weekly newspaper published by W.C. Walker; Alex Brown Meat Market; and at the end of the block, Ehret Brothers (Chris & Carl) General Merchandise Store.

MAIN ST. REDMOND. CENTRAL ORE.

DOUGLAS COUNTY

The town of Dillard in Douglas County is located south of Roseburg. Here a group of townspeople stand in front of the General Merchandise Store on October 25, 1908. Postmaster and proprietor of the store, Luther E. Milledge, is in the center of the photo holding a small child in his arms. Others in the photo area: M.F. Howard; G.W. Gage; J.H. Younce; J.A. Eggers; G.B. Laurance and son; Mr. Green and Mr. Coon. The rest are unknown.

The post office for the town of Nugget in about 1905 in the gold mining area of Douglas County, located about twelve miles east of Myrtle Creek. The man seated in the photo is believed to be Benjamin F. Saunders, the first postmaster of Nugget.

GILLIAM COUNTY

This scene portrays the annual harvest for farmers in Gilliam County, where heavy combines were pulled by thirty-two horses. The large stands of wheat which blow in the winds from the Columbia River account for this central Oregon county being called "The Golden Land."

Benjamin Arthur Gifford, one of Oregon's itinerant photographers, stops at Robbers' Roost approaching Condon on Thirty-Mile Canyon. Gifford *(standing near wagon with his hand in his pocket)* had a caravan of photographers consisting of two buggies and a wagon serving as a darkroom. His assistant, Charles Y. Lamb *(right)*, looks down on the group.

GRANT COUNTY

Prairie City is located about
fifteen miles east of Canyon
City on the John Day River.
Notice the Sumpter Valley
trackage into the city and the
railroad yards *(left)*.

The Sumpter Valley Railroad station with Agent Ed Hibbs standing in front of the building. The area above the station was living quarters for Hibbs and his family. The car in the photo is a 1920 Dodge touring car. Today the tracks are gone, but the building is still standing and houses a museum.

A 1910 caravan of new 1909 E.M.F. automobiles being shown to the people of Prairie City. It is believed they were shipped by rail to Baker City and from this point, caravaned through various cities in Central Oregon endeavoring to sell these new cars. To encourage sales and interest, women were taught to drive. We were unable to determine if this actually resulted in an increase in car sales. Mrs. Lillian Sinnett and Sible Knapp are shown at the wheel of the "right-hand drive" cars. Others in the photo are: M. Durkeimer, John L. Stalker, D.A. McFadden, Donald Ross, F.W. Peet, F.M. Stewart and F.S. Reider. The E.F.M. automobile company was started by three men: Mr. Everett, Mr. Metzer, and Mr. Flaunders. This company was sold in 1913 to the Studebaker Auto Company.

HARNEY COUNTY

Burns is the county seat for Harney County, the largest county in the state. A Fourth of July celebration in 1894 is being held at the opening of the new courthouse. Attending the ceremony are *(left to right)*: I.S. Geer; County Commissioners Ad Marks and Rudolph Sitz; Judge Rutherford; Tom Jones; Leon Brown; Mr. De Witt; Captain A.W. Gowarn; Sheriff Gittings; Mrs. Gittings; Mrs. Ollie B. Robinson; Deputy County Clerk Rose Hembrey; County Clerk Charles Kenyon; Mrs. John Vaughn; Deputy Sheriff John Vaughn; James Gittings; Frank Miller; Mrs. Maurice Fitzgerald and baby; Ed Stauffer. On the balcony is Frank Smith. The two children on the steps are Jack and Jennie Lee Robinson.

HOOD RIVER COUNTY

Lt. Oakley G. Kelly made the first flight by air over the top of Mount Hood, altitude 11,225 feet, in 1924 with a 400–horsepower Liberty engine-powered De Haviland twin-cockpit biplane. This was the "backbone" ship of the 321st Observation Squadron stationed at Vancouver, Washington, of which Kelly was the commanding officer. This trip was the first time Mount Hood had been photographed from the air.

Mitchell Point Tunnel in Hood River County on the Columbia River Highway overlooking the Union Pacific tracks, with an afternoon passenger train heading west. This tunnel is now a tomb. Its entrance was closed in 1954 and filled with stone and mortar so that the water grade highway could be built.

CLUB BREAKFASTS
NO SUBSTITUTIONS

No. 1 ....*25c*

Toast, with Jelly or Marmalade
Cup Coffee

No. 3 ....*50c*

Choice of Baked Apple, Sliced Ba-
nana, Stewed Prunes or Juice of
Tomato, Grapefruit or Pineapple
Hot or Cold Cereal with Cream
Wheat or Buckwheat Cakes with
Ham, Bacon or Sausage, or
Fried Cornmeal Mush with Ham,
Bacon or Sausage or Two Eggs,
any style, with Toast
Coffee

No. 2 ....*35c*

Choice of Stewed Prunes, Sliced
Banana, Baked Apple, Tomato Juice,
Canned Grapefruit

Toast, with Jelly or Marmalade

Cup Coffee

No. 4 ....*60c*

Choice of Fruit in Season
Hot or Cold Cereal with Cream
Ham or Bacon or Sausage with Eggs

Toast

Coffee

See Bonneville Dam—24 miles.

LUNCHEON

Club luncheons are served at prices ranging from 50c to $1.00, consisting of

Cocktail or Soup
Entree or Roast from Special Menu
Potatoes   Vegetables
Salad
Bread and Butter
Dessert   Drink

Price of entree or roast on special menu is price of luncheon

---

Travel the Magnificent Columbia River Highway in Daylight.
You will always regret it, if you fail to see it.

DINNER

Club dinners are served at prices ranging from 75c to $1.00, consisting of

Relish
Cocktail or Soup
Entree or Roast from Special Menu
Potatoes   Vegetable
Salad
Bread and Butter
Dessert   Drink

The price of entree or roast on special menu is price of dinner.

Special Steak or Chicken Dinner—$1.25

Menu from the Columbia Gorge Hotel. Henri Thiele, who for many years
was chief steward of the Benson Hotel in Portland, was made manager of the
hotel. In the 1920s these meals were considered expensive.

The Columbia Gorge Hotel, located roughly two miles west of Hood River, was opened in June, 1921, shortly after the Columbia River Highway had been paved from Portland to The Dalles. The hotel was built by Simon Benson, the lumber king, who was a firm believer that the Columbia River Highway was America's greatest and most-scenic highway. He felt Oregonians deserved the same greatness in a hotel— that one complemented the other. It was built some 150 feet above the Columbia River and contained forty-eight rooms on a seventy-four-acre tract.

The Bridge of the Gods is a steel cantilever bridge built in 1926 spanning the Columbia River west of the city of Cascade Locks. Below is UP No. 106, the City of Portland, traveling eastbound through the Columbia Gorge on the Oregon side of the river enroute to Chicago. Thousands of years ago the Indians believed a bridge of stone extended across the river at the same location. In the background is Shell Rock, a portion of the Cascade Range mountains. In 1927, Colonel Charles A. Lindbergh, on his first trip to the Pacific Northwest, flew the *Spirit of St. Louis* (his plane) underneath this bridge which is only 135 feet above the water.

JACKSON COUNTY

Siskiyou is a small community in Jackson County high in the hills of the Siskiyou Mountains. This photo taken in 1929 shows one of the powerful steam locomotives of that day reaching the top of the hill. The train is pulled by a double-header (two locomotives) used because of the steep grade. The helper lead engine is a 4300–class locomotive (4-8-2). Between Hilt, California and Siskiyou, this train has climbed 1,208 feet in thirty-four minutes. Notice the arm of the train order board is in a lowered position, signaling to the conductor that he can pass through without stopping. If the arm was in a horizontal position the train would either come to a stop or receive train orders "on the fly" before proceeding.

The railroad between the states of Oregon and California was completed in 1887. The Oregon & Californian Railroad had built south as far as Ashland, Oregon, while the Southern Pacific Railroad had built north to Hornbrook, California. A twenty-nine mile horse-drawn stage trip handled all passengers, freight, and U.S. Mail between these two rail points, which was the most treacherous portion of the trip as it crossed the Siskiyou Mountains. This old photo shows the California, Oregon & Idaho Stage Company in 1887 making its last trip before the rail line was completed connecting the Oregon and California lines. The stage is at Barron's Station, located on the H.F. Barron's stock ranch, about six miles south of Ashland in Jackson County. This was the last stop before the stage entered California. Daniel Cailey drove the horses on the last trip.

"The Siskiyou Mountains are the border guardians between California and Oregon. Scenically they are not eclipsed by any other upraised part of the American outdoors. Yet their grandeur is not their only appeal. Geologically these summits present one of the most interesting passages in the history of our globe. The Siskiyou summits constitute one of the oldest patches of dry land on the face of the earth. They were growing a forest when the greater part of Europe was still beneath the water. They were the hillocks of a low, flat island a hundred miles in length when the Pacific Ocean reached eastward to the Rocky Mountains." (From a Southern Pacific publication—1955)

JEFFERSON COUNTY

Madras is the county seat of Jefferson County. This 1912 photo taken in front of the Oregon Trunk railroad station shows a White touring car belonging to Howard W. Turner, the first mayor of the city. He is at the wheel, while his family walks on the station platform.

JOSEPHINE COUNTY

The Wolf Creek Tavern in the small hamlet of Wolf Creek was built in 1857, two years before Oregon became a state. This historical structure was one of the stops for the Overland Mail Route running between Portland and Sacramento. This horse-drawn stage operation continued until 1887 when the railroad between Oregon and California was completed. Note the reasonable prices for meals and lodging in the 1930s. A 1929 Ford Model A sports coupe is parked near the side of the building.

Laurel Camp at Wolf Creek, Oregon, in the 1920s was a campsite for passing motorists and a stage stopping point. It had a post office, along with a steak house and a garage that handled Union Gasoline. A 1926 Ford Model T coupe *(left)* and a Fageol Pacific Greyhound stage *(right)* are shown.

KLAMATH COUNTY

The city of Klamath Falls in the southern Oregon county of Klamath in 1929 celebrates the opening of a new transcontinental rail line from Portland to the East. This photo shows part of the parade taken on South Sixth Street looking northeast at Plumb Ridge and Hogsback Mountain *(background)*. Notice the Hupmobile touring car *(left)* with James Alma Ormandy and Robert E. Kelly, Southern Pacific officials, sitting in the front seat. The car directly behind it is a 1922 Ford Model T Coach, and the car to the extreme right, with just the rear showing, is a 1925 Chevrolet touring car.

The trains must go through! This is a typical winter scene in the Cascades of Klamath County. A rotary fan wheel whirling at a great velocity cuts through the snow throwing it far to the side of the track. Snow in this area has averaged as much as a foot-an-hour, and along with high winds, blizzards, and sub-zero temperatures, keeping the rail line open is often a real problem.

LAKE COUNTY

The city of Lakeview, with an elevation of 4800 feet, has the distinction of being the tallest town in Oregon as it has the highest elevation of any incorporated area along the Oregon highway system. This city serves as the county seat for Lake County. This photo taken before 1900 shows Water street, now called "E" street, looking north. Most of these buildings were destroyed by fire at the beginning of the century.

The front of the Lakeview General Land Office on October 26, 1907 where 224 people line up to file claims on U.S. Federal Reserve lands to be opened to the public the next day. It is believed this was the last "line-up" for public lands in the state. The photo was taken looking north on Center Street. Some of those pictured are:

1. Aldred McCoul
2. Mrs. Bable
3. Mrs. Jim McShane
4. George Harper
5. Bill Casebeer
6. Jim McShane
7. Irving Casebeer
8. Robert Weir
9. W.E. Anderson
10. Frank Moran
11. Josie Harvey
12. Hotel Bartender
13. George Storkman
14. "Fat" Malor
15. Judge Charles Tonningsen
16. L.F. Conn
17. J.N. Watson, Registrar of General Land Office in Lakeview
18. C.V. Snider Buildings:
19. The Odd Fellows Building
20. Livery Stable
21. The Wilcox Building

LANE COUNTY

The Mapleton daily stage in 1900, ready for the sixty mile trip to Eugene, all in Lane County. The trip goes along the upper waters of the Siuslaw River through the rich timber sections and over the divide to reach its destination. Joe Morris, Jr., the agent for the Eugene Elmira & Mapleton Stage Line, is standing in the entrance of his General Merchandise Store. He also served as postmaster and his son, Norman G. Morris, assistant postmaster, is seen standing beside him. The driver is believed to be William C. Hamilton.

A 1916 Knott fire engine parked in front of the City Hall in Eugene. The firemen are: Chief William E. Nusbaum *(in uniform)*; others are: Dale Croner, Henry Weber, Pennington and Hendershott.

THE EUGENE CITY REGISTER.

VOL. 2.　　　EUGENE CITY, OREGON, WEDNESDAY, OCT. 21, 1885.　　　No. 3.

ENTERED AT EUGENE CITY P. O.,
AS SECOND CLASS MATTER.

"A GOVERNMENT OF THE PEOPLE BY THE PEOPLE AND FOR THE PEOPLE."

PRICE TWO DOL-
LARS PER YEAR.

Eugene City Register.

HODSON & YORAN, Proprietors.

[Published every Wednesday.]

Office: N. W. corner Olive and Eight Sts.

RATES OF SUBSCRIPTION:
One year $2.00
Special rates to agents on application.

RATES OF ADVERTISING:

STEAM PRINTING

STATE AND COUNTY OFFICIALS.

State Officials.

County Officials.

City Officials.

School Board.

Churches.

A MARKED YOUTH.

Years ago there lived in the interior of New York a boy, the son
of a farmer, who also worked at the
trade of a potter. The boy was a
marked youth, because he would do
with might whatever he undertook.
He was a leader in the ordinary
sports of boyhood, and whenever
the farm or the pottery relaxed their
hold upon him he would be found
repairing some damaged article or
devising a new implement.

His father was poor; the farm was
small, and could only be enlarged
by clearing up the primeval forest.
The boy was anxious to acquire
knowledge, but his services were so
necessary to his father that he
could not be spared to attend the
winter term of the common school.

But the boy was in earnest. With
the aid of his brother, one year his
junior, he chopped and cleared four
acres of birch and maple woodland,
plowed it, planted it with corn, har-
vested the crop, and then asked, as
his compensation to be allowed to
attend school during the winter. Of
course the father granted his wish.

When the boy was seventeen, the
father's pottery business had so increased as to demand a more exten-
sive factory. A carpenter was hired
to build the building, and the boy
assisted him. So familiar did he
become with the tools and the trade
that he determined, with the aid of
the younger brother, to erect a two-
story frame dwelling-house for his
father's family. The two boys cut
the timber from the forest, planned
and framed the structure, and then
invited the neighbors to assist at
the "raising." They came from far
and near to see what a lad of seventeen had done. When every mort-
ice and tenon was found to fit its
place, and the frame was seen to
stand perfect and secure, the veterans cheered the young architect and

INDIAN TRADITION OF THE CREATION.

The Pottawattamie tribes held, as
did many other divisions of the race,
a theory of origin not unlike the
Bible account of the "Creation and
Deluge." They believed in a Great
Spirit, Kitchemonedo, and an evil
spirit, Matchemonedo—the one ben-
eficient, good; the other the immediate cause of all sickness, sorrow,
suffering, wrong in life. Believing
them to be nearly equal in power
they propitiated both, but the greater number looked upon Kitchemonedo as the true spirit, all powerful
and creative. He made a world and
filled it with men and women, and
then because they forgot to lift up
their eyes and thank him, he plunged
his world into a lake and drowned
them all. He then took his world
out of the water and hung it up to
dry, and made one very handsome
man, who, after dwelling alone for
a time, grew very lonesome, "oh, so
lonesome," that Kitchemonedo sent
him a sister. This cheered him for
many years, when he grew lonesome
again and wished Kitchemonedo had
sent him some other man's sister;
accordingly he dreamed a dream
and told it to his sister. "Five
young men will come to your lodge
to-night. The Great Spirit says
you must not speak to the first four,
but run to the fifth and laugh and
greet him."

The first Usama, or tobacco, came
smiling upon her, was gruffly re-
pulsed, and sank down and died upon the spot. The second, Wapko,
or pumpkin, met the same fate. The
third, Eshkossimin, or melon, and
the fourth, Kokees, or bean, expired
before her scornful face at the very
door-way of her lodge, but when
Mondamin, or maize came, she flew
to meet him. A joyful reception
followed, a wedding feast sprang up

TO PREVENT "CROWS' FEET."

T. G. E. asks a preventive for
"crows' feet" that so insidiously
creep about the outer angle of the
eyes. I fear they will come and
are not to be banished; still they
may be ameliorated. Only the finest linen or cambric wash cloth
should be used for the face and only
soft water. At night bathe the face
with hot water, and apply some cold
cream or pure olive oil to the wrinkles. Never use a flesh towel for
the face; only the most delicate fab-
rics should be employed. Keep
regular hours, remember that "early
to bed and early to rise" will keep
crows' feet from tormenting the
eyes.

I know an old lady of 70 whose
complexion is as fair and free from
wrinkles as a little child's. She says
she has never bathed her face with
anything harsher than a linen handkerchief. With regard to the eyes
a suggestion may not be out of place
here. Always bathe them toward
the nose. By this means the sight
is improved and the chances for
"crows' feet" are lessened. When
the eyes become tired just try gently bathing or simply making passes
over the eyes toward the nose and
find how soothing the result will be.

THE DEEPEST WELL IN THE WORLD.

The deepest well in the world is
located at Homewood, Pa. It is
owned by George Westinghouse, Jr.
The average depth of the Homewood wells is about 1,850 feet. In
the well now drilling everything
found of the nature of gas or water
at a depth of 2,000 feet was cast off
as unimportant, and the drill at present is said to be a little over 6,000
feet below the surface, which would
make it by all odds the deepest well

THE GUARD.

VOL. 1.　　　EUGENE CITY, OREGON, SATURDAY, JULY 13, 1867.　　　NO. 7.

THE GUARD.

PUBLISHED EVERY SATURDAY,
BY
J. B. ALEXANDER.

TERMS—Three dollars a year, invariably
in advance.

Rates of Advertising—Legal, and other
transient advertisements, will be charged at
the rate of $2.50 per square for the first inser-
tion and, $1.00 for each subsequent insertion.
Twelve lines or less of Minion type counted a
square.

A liberal deduction from the above rates
made to persons advertising by the year.

The number of insertions must be marked on
all transient advertisements or they will be
continued until ordered out, and charged for
accordingly.

BELL & DEXTER,
BOOKSELLERS and STATIONERS
636 CLAY STREET,
SAN FRANCISCO, CALIFORNIA.

GENERAL AGENTS for American and Foreign Magazines, Newspapers and other
Periodicals. Importers and Dealers in Books
and Stationery of every description, Law books,
Blank books, and School books.

Newspapers, Magazines, Reviews, Medical
and Scientific Journals, or either Periodicals published in any part of the World, will be furnished to order. A circular will be sent on request
giving a more extended list of Magazines and
Papers, with the price annexed. The following
are some of the most popular:
PER YEAR.

TRAIN ON FINANCE.

The following is an extract from a
speech delivered in the Gold Room of
Geo. Francis Train. Mr Train was called
upon for a speech and he gave them his
views without any reserve. The people
will do well to hear what Wall street says
and prepare for a near and terrible storm.
After reviewing the financial condition of
the country from 1861 to the present time
and contrasting our situation then and
now he supposes the crisis to be here
and says:

"Then comes the rush on National
banks for greenbacks, and the greenbacks
are not there. (Sensation.) What is
the result? Does Congress help us? No
—the lawyers are in power; what do they
care? They add $600,000,000 bounty to
the debt, and advance their own salaries
to $5,000! In the South to be admitted
under the Military Bill? No; the team
holds the reins. Where, then, are we
floating? Congress saw McCulloch has
made a mistake; and it is an administration blunder, the Jacobins intend to pass
no bill of relief. They will pinch the
country this year and bring on a financial
crash in the fall—(remember this is the
panic year of the never-failing seven)—
lay it on the Administration policy, and
when every body is broken, Congress will
meet in the winter and pass Randall's bill,
putting greenbacks in the place of the
$300,000,000 National bank bill. Pass
another bill paying duties on imports in
greenbacks, and then another bill paying
interest on the $1,400,000,000 five-twen-
ties in legal tenders. In other words,
give the country one currency—that is,
twenty-five hundred millions of legal tenders, instead of sixteen currencies as at
present. (Applause.) This makes all
happy for the Presidential elections of
1868. Delirium tremens requires National
whiskey to recuperate the system. The
next war is to be financial. Land and labor against banks and bondholders; and
the former own the notes. The South
had no debt. The West little. The
greenback saves wiped off their mortgages,
and placed the load on the back of the
bondholders. The debt, rests uneasily on
the seashore and in Europe, and the shadow is on the wall.

Paying gold interest to greenbacks in
repudiation you say. Why so? nearly all
the States have done it. New York taking

THE STATE REPUBLICAN.

DEVOTED TO THE POLITICAL AND GENERAL INTERESTS OF THE PEOPLE.

VOL. II.   EUGENE CITY, OREGON, APRIL 4, 1863.   NO. 12.

THE STATE REPUBLICAN.

Published every Saturday by

J. NEWTON GALE.

Terms of Subscription.

The Republican will be published at $3 50 a year in advance; $3 00 if paid at the end of six months; or $4 00 at the close of the year. One dollar additional will be charged for each year payment is neglected.

No papers discontinued until all arrearages are paid, except at our option.

Rates of Advertising.

One square (ten lines or less) one month..........

STAMP DUTIES.

THE LAW OF NEWSPAPERS.

THE REBEL PIRATE.

THE OREGON STATE JOURNAL.

The Oregon State Journal.

VOL. 13.   EUGENE CITY, OREGON, SATURDAY, NOVEMBER 4, 1876.   NO. 39.

OREGON STATE JOURNAL.
PUBLISHED EVERY SATURDAY.
H. R. KINCAID,
EDITOR AND PROPRIETOR.
Office on Ninth Street.

Terms of Subscription.
One Year, $3 00; Six Months, $2 00; Three Months, $1 50.—In Advance.

Rates of Advertising.

ATTORNEYS.

G. B. DORRIS,

ATTORNEY & COUNSELOR-AT-LAW

EUGENE CITY, OREGON.

PHYSICIANS.

DR. GEO. W. ODELL,

DR. JOSEPH P. GILL,

DR. A. W. PATTERSON,

Office opposite St. Charles Hotel,
AND ALSO AT RESIDENCE,
EUGENE CITY, OREGON.

Drs. Nicklin & Shields,

TILDEN TO TWEED.

THE NEW LAWS.

SENATE BILLS.

REBEL WAR CLAIMS.

THE DANGER TO BE FEARED IN CASE OF DEMOCRATIC SUCCESS.

HARD TIMES.

LINCOLN COUNTY

The daily stage running over the Corvallis & Yaquina Bay Wagon Road between Corvallis and Elk City handled the U.S. Mail and passengers before the coming of the railroad. The remainder of the trip from Elk City to the various points along Yaquina Bay, including Newport, was by water via the Yaquina River. This entire area was in Benton County until 1893 when the county was divided and the coastal area became Lincoln County.

An advertisement appearing in August, 1884, gives full particulars for the fifty-three mile trip via stage from Corvallis to Elk City and the twenty-two mile water trip from Elk City to Newport or Yaquina Bay points.

All Aboard! Making the three mile trip along the beach from Newport to Agate Beach in a 1908 Packard are *(left to right)*: Edith Hendry; Ina Irvin Daugherty, wife of Warren Daugherty (President of the Daugherty Lumber Company); and Ana Allen Cordon, wife of Guy Cordon (a U.S. senator from Oregon).

The Agate Beach Inn, located three miles north of Newport in Lincoln County, was built in the early 1900s and burned to the ground in 1948. It could lodge sixty-two guests and was managed by Mrs. Katherine George. In front of the inn notice the trackage and "cross-buck" of the Yaquina Northern Railroad. This railroad was built by the U.S. government during World War I for a rail connection with the Southern Pacific at Yaquina City. Large stands of spruce logs growing in the coastal area were cut and shipped over the government railroad to be used for building airplanes during WWI.

Samuel Glasgow Irvin leans against the fence of his new home, built in 1890. It was the first home in the Nye Beach area of Newport. His wife, May Francis Ball, is standing on the porch, while his three daughters, Alda May Irvin, Lola Lydia Irvin (Ormandy), and Ina Naomi Irvin (Daugherty) are shown in front. Irvin came to Newport in 1881 and purchased then developed one hundred and sixty acres of land in the vicinity of Nye Creek. He followed the teaching profession, served as county school superintendent, and was the mayor of Newport for several terms.

Samuel Irvin added an extension to his home in 1905, and as a result of the heavy coastal tourist traffic, he converted his home into the Irvin House Hotel. He attended the Lewis & Clark Centennial in Portland that same year and was so impressed with the Forestry Building that upon his return to Newport he constructed the Log Cabin Inn and Oasis Lunch Parlor, located about two hundred feet east of the hotel. This photo is of his family and other important Newport people on hand for the grand opening. The Irvin House was later sold to J.W. Kelly & Sons and renamed the Hotel Kelly.

Swimmers with rented bathing suits from the Newport Beach Natatorium in about 1910. Swimmers could either swim inside the Nat in the warm heated pool, go outside and lie in the warm sands on the beach, or jump in the chilly Pacific Ocean. All in all, it was grand fun! In the background is the Nicolai Hotel *(center)* and the Natatorium *(right)*.

A family enjoying Newport beach in July, 1912.

Nothing was more refreshing or enjoyable than feeling the cool breeze from the ocean currents on a nice, warm day at the beach. Here is a group looking for agates and other pretty stones. These people look like they were dressed for church, rather than a carefree day along Newport beach—but this *was* 1910.

Helen Fulton Thompkins playing in the sand at Newport on a nice warm day. How old is she? All we know is that she graduated from Oregon Agriculture College (now Oregon State University) in 1892.

The *Yaquina Bay News* office in Newport in about 1905. William Matthews. the editor, is in the center of the photo. Note the cordwood beside the building used for fuel to keep the office warm.

Yaquina Bay Post.

VOL. I. NEWPORT, YAQUINA BAY, OREGON. JUNE 7, 1882. NO. 2

Farmer's Hymn

BY JOHN G WHITTIER.

O painter of fruits and flowers,
We own thy wise design.
Whereby these human hands of ours
May share the work of Thine.

Apart from Thee we plant in vain
The root and sow the seed;
Thy early and thy later rain,
Thy sun and dew we need.

Our soil is sweet with thankfulness,
Our burden is our boon;
The curse of earth's gray morning is
The blessing of its noon.

Why search the wide world ev'rywhere
For Eden's unknown ground.
That garden of the primal pair
May never more be found.

But, blessed by Thee, our parental toil
May right the ancient ground,
And give to every clime and soil
The beauty lost so long.

and look homestead flowers and fruited
how to cate
Eden's orchard shame;
Election te the tempting sweets of these
only a fe ke Eve without her blame.

for a ch North, the South, the East and
gave sa West,
ates. The pride of every zone,
The fairest, rarest and the best
May all be made our own.

Its earliest shrines the young world sought
In hill-groves and in bowers;
The fittest offering thither brought
Were thine own fruits and flowers.

And still with reverent hands we cull
Thy gifts each year renewed;
The good is always beautiful,
The beautiful is good.

The Rolling Stone.

I do not see how we can move the first of April. It will be dreadfully hard."

"Oh, I will hire some one to help pack; but I really think it would be better for us. You need not lift a finger about moving."

Hattie Bradley had learned before this time that when William "crooked his elbow" nothing could bend it, so she said no more on the subject—and in a few days her husband told her he had hired the Kendrick farm, and got it a hundred dollars cheaper than the one they occupied. They must vacate their present home the last of March, as the new tenant would want to take possession then.

Of course there was nothing more to be said, but when packing up came there was no one to be had to assist, and Mrs. Bradley had the whole thing to do herself. She was a careful housewife, and took every precaution to have the furniture protected from injury in transporting; but the roads were rough, and the sled that had her nice chamber set upon it upset, and the bedstead got smashed and marred, the large mirror smashed and the back was broken off the little rocking chair. The cook stove had one of the oven doors broken, and one leg was lost, and plenty of

leave, even if he does not sell it; it it a hard farm to work."

"William, 'a rolling stone gathers no moss;' it was a great damage to us moving last year, aside from my sickness. My furniture was broken and ruined and not a thing has been mended yet."

"I never think of it when I have time to do it; to tell the truth, Hattie I have half a mind to give up farming and turn my hand at something else."

"What else can you earn a living by?"

"There's plenty of work a man to do, and I think I should have more money at the end of the year even if I worked out by the day."

"But your stock—you have a dairy now."

"Cows will sell," said shortly, and left the room, while his poor wife sat down for a good

Nothing more was of the change for some days, and Hattie began to think her husband decided to stay where they were. When at last he told her that he had concluded to move again, she begged him to make some arangement with Kendrick so that at least I could stay one year more. "Keck will lease the farm, if I want it. I want to live where I can ear ore and you

Brother Gardner's Philosophy.

"I war cleanin' off de sidewalk de odder day," observed the old man as the meeting opened, "when 'long cum a man who war achin' fur somebody to knock him known. He didn't 'zactly know what to say to begin a fuss, but he finally made out to remark dat if he war Mayor ob dis city he'd run all de niggers into de ribber. I felt it my duty to bring de snow-shovel down on top his head, an' he drapped. He stayed drapped fur about five minutes, an', when he got up an' pursued his way, his opinyuns seemed to have undergone a great change. I spoke of dis bekase I want ebery member ob dis club to realize dat de only rule wort libin' by am dat which uses men jist as day use you. Try to lib by any oder rule an' you will be cheated, swindled robbed, an' abused ebery week in de y'ar. De man who thinks he has sufficient provocashun to kick you will feel a contempt fur you if you doan' kick back. De man who robs you expects to be dealt wid as a robber. Deal wid him as an angel an' he would sneer at you. No man has a right to expect better treatment dan he am willin' to bestow, an' few do expect it." Let's go an' console some ob de

A Fish Story.

A man has an artificial pond with at least 3,000 fish, each weighing from half a pound to two pounds, more or less. He also has a little girl, 5 years old, who has succeeded in training the fish so that she can go to the edge of the pond, and with a handful of crumbs feed them from her chubby hand. They have learned to jump out of the water and snatch worms from her fingers, and they are extremely fond of their little mistress. One day she lost her balance, and pitched headlong into the water where it was deep. She says that when she went "away down," she called lustily for help. Her cries quickly attracted her parents, and they were horrified at seeing the little girl floating upon the surface of the pond. The father rushed to the water's edge and reached out for his pet, and as he raised her from the water a perfectly solid mass of trout was found beneath her. These faithful subjects of the little queen, as she fell, quickly gathered beneath her, and thus showed their love for their mistress by holding up her body until aid arrived, thus preventing her from meeting a watery grave.—*Whitehall Times.*

YAQUINA BAY NEWS.

VOL. XXXI NEWPORT, LINCOLN COUNTY, ORE., December 6, 1923. No 42.

Coolidge Wins In South Dakota Primary

First Nomination Of the 1924 Campaign

Pierre, S. D., Dec. 5.—South Dakota today leads all other states of the Union in the selection of a list of candidates for the 1924 presidential elections.

Here is the ticket adopted by the Republican party:

For President, Calvin C. Coolidge; for vice president, Senator Arthur Capper, Kansas; for U. S. senator, Governor W. H. Mo- Masters of South Dakota.

The Democrats endorsed:

For president, W. G. McAdoo; for vice president, James W. Gerard of New York City.

Hard Gale Hits Bay

One of the hardest southwest gales that has ever been experienced in this portion of the coast set in early Wednesday evening and raged furiously throughout the night accompanied by a heavy rainfall. The surf along the ocean beach was running mountains high and the tide reached past the 11 foot mark on the tide

Astoria Bootleggers Guilty

Hotel Proprietors Convicted in 15 Minutes

Astoria, Dec. 6.—The government won its first battle with Astoria bootleggers when Sam and Antone Skojo, proprietors of the Gold Star hotel, were convicted 15 minutes after the jury in Federal Judge Bean's court received the case yesterday.

Each was convicted on three counts, sale of liquor, possession, and maintaining of a nuisance. The men will be sentenced at 10 o'clock this morning, but received five days in which to file a motion for a new trial, which will serve to postpone execution of the sentence. Their bond was increased from $500 each to $1000 each.

The case was the first of a large number which the state plans to turn over to the government because of prolonged delays due to red tape in the courts. Closing of the Gold Star hotel as a result of the verdict was declared to be assured by prohibition enforcement officers.

THE ROCK QUARRY.

ENGINEER LOSES LEG

Manary Logging Camp is Scene Of Another Accident

George Morgan, an engineer at the Manary logging camp near Waldport had the misfortune to meet with an accident Saturday in which he lost his left leg. In some manner he got caught between the logging engine and a log and his leg was so badly crushed that immediate amputation was necessary. It was taken off above the knee, Dr. Belt of Newport and Dr. Roberts of Waldport performing the operation.

The injured man was brought here and taken out to the Corvallis General Hospital, the hospital ambulance coming over for him.

Examinations for Army Appointments

1. An examination of applicants for appointment as commissioned officers in the Medical Corps of the Regular Army will be held in the Ninth Corps Area (covering the PacificCoast states) during the period January 21, 25th, 1923.

2. To be eligible for appointment the applicant must be be-

South Beach Dock Has Waiting Room

At last people can await the coming and going of the ferry boats at the South Beach dock without being obliged to stand out in the weather. A waiting room has been built onto the dock ware room. The Port of Newport supplied the material and the South Beach people donated the construction work.

Coleman On Basket Ball Team

Oregon Agricultural College, Corvallis, Dec. 4.—Edward Coleman of Newport, Sophomore in commerce, will go on the preseason barnstorming tour of the college basket ball team during the Christmas holidays.

Games will be played at San Francisco, Oakland, San Jose, Stockton, and Fresno. Although the entire schedule is not definitely arranged it is thought that the team will go on south to meet the Los Angeles Athletic club and Hollywood Athletic club teams.

While in Southern California the Beaver players will attend the annual intersectional football game at Pasadena. This game will be on New Year's day, and will be between the Annapolis

can tell that a man is wearing a navy blue suit and a black hat.

The new plant produces a direct current which is most ideal for pictures.

There is no flicker, just a flood of pure white light with nothing to strain the eyes.

50,000 MEN NEEDED TO FILL GAPS IN U. S. ARMY

Stringent Entrance Requirements Keep Down Enlistments.

Washington.—Reductions in the commissioned and enlisted strength of the army resulting from congressional action have brought two extremely difficult problems to War department chiefs for solutions that have not been found, Maj. Gen. Robert C. Davis, adjutant general of the army, declared in his annual report made public here.

"The effect of the enforced reduction in the commissioned strength," he said, "has been far-reaching. It has been found impossible to carry into anything like full effect the program for national defense included in the national defense act approved June 4, 1920."

Regarding the enlisted strength of the army, the report said:

"The small pay of the recruit and the remarkably high wages paid for labor of all kinds throughout the United States have greatly discouraged enlistment, but since the close of the fiscal year another obstacle has arisen equally serious. In the act making appropriations for the War department for the fiscal year ending June 30, 1924, the following appears:

"That no part of the funds herein appropriated shall be utilized for recruiting or enlistment, unless the applicant furnishes a birth certificate or the affidavit of two disinterested

Auto Registration In Oregon 165,042

Salem, Or., Dec. 1.—A total of 165,042 automobiles had been registered in the automobile department of the secretary of state's office here up to closing time November 30. This is an increase of more than 30,000 over the total registration of 1922, when 134,566 automobiles carried Oregon tags. Secretary of State Kozer estimates that registrations for 1924, which are already coming in, will reach 180,000. Receipts of the department to date total $4,656,481.87.

Taxpayers Hold Meeting

Organization Was Formed

At a meeting of taxpayers of Lincoln county held at Toledo on December 1st, 1923, a temporary organization was had with W. H. Osburn as chairman and Henry Howell as secretary.

There being a small attendance the meeting was adjourned to meet at the court house on Friday, the 14th of December, 1923, at 1:30 p. m. Notice to be given in the county newspapers.

Over three hundred taxpayers

Newport volunteer firemen pose with their new "hand-pumper" fire engine in 1909 in front of the unfinished city hall. Newport secured this used engine from Walla Walla, Washington. It was built in 1880 by Rumsey & Company at Seneca Falls, New York. Some of the firemen are: Herbert F. Jenkins (dry goods and jeweler); Charles H. Bradshaw (photographer); William M. Berry (dentist); Louis C. Smith (real estate); Frank J. Blattner (shoe store); Vivian Cartwright (confectionery store); Frank Lane (postmaster); William Mathers (publisher, *Yaquina Bay News*). The young men in the background are unknown.

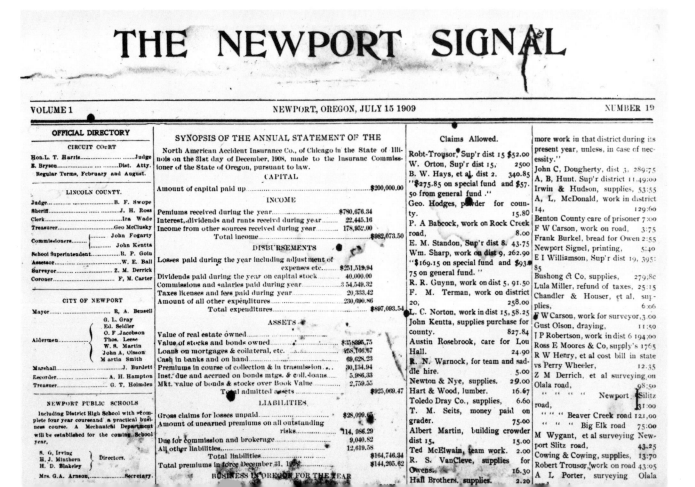

THE NEWPORT SIGNAL

VOLUME 1   NEWPORT, OREGON, JULY 15 1909   NUMBER 19

OFFICIAL DIRECTORY

CIRCUIT COURT

Hon. L. T. Harris..................Judge
E. Bryson.................Dist. Atty.
Regular Terms, February and August.

LINCOLN COUNTY.

Judge........................B. F. Swope
Sheriff.......................J. H. Ross
Clerk.........................Ira Wade
Treasurer...............Geo McClusky
Commissioners....{ John Fogarty
                  { John Kentta
School Superintendent.....R. P. Goin
Assessor...................W. E. Ball
Surveyor.................Z. M. Derrick
Coroner..................F. M. Carter

CITY OF NEWPORT

Mayor......................R. A. Bensell
Aldermen....{ G. L. Gray
            { Ed. Seidler
            { O. F. Jacobson
            { Thos. Leese
            { W. S. Martin
            { John A. Olson
            { Martin Smith
Marshal......................J. Burdett
Recorder................A. H. Hampton
Treasurer...............G. T. Holmden

NEWPORT PUBLIC SCHOOLS

Including District High School with complete four year course and a practical business course. A Mechanical Department will be established for the coming School year.

S. G. Irving }
H. J. Minthorn } Directors.
H. D. Blakeley }

Mrs. G. A. Arnson..............Secretary.

SYNOPSIS OF THE ANNUAL STATEMENT OF THE

North American Accident Insurance Co., of Chicago in the State of Illinois on the 31st day of December, 1908, made to the Insurance Commissioner of the State of Oregon, pursuant to law.

CAPITAL

Amount of capital paid up..............................$200,000.00

INCOME

Pemiums received during the year...............$780,676.34
Interest, dividends and rents received during year.. 22,445.16
Income from other sources received during year.... 178,952.00
    Total income..............................$982,073.50

DISBURSEMENTS

Losses paid during the year including adjustment of expenses etc.....$251,519.94
Dividends paid during the year on capital stock.... 40,000.00
Commissions and salaries paid during year......3 54,549.32
Taxes licenses and fees paid during year......... 20,333.42
Amount of all other expenditures.................230,690.86
    Total expenditures...................$897,093.54

ASSETS

Value of real estate owned........................
Value of stocks and bonds owned..........$358,395.75
Loans on mortgages & collateral, etc. 458,166.67
Cash in banks and on hand................... 69,628.23
Premiums in course of collection & in transmission... 30,134.94
Inst. due and accrued on bonds mtgs. & coll. loans.. 5,986.33
Mkt. value of bonds & stocks over Book Value...... 2,759.55
    Total admitted assets...................$925,069.47

LIABILITIES

Gross claims for losses unpaid.................. $28,099.65
Amount of unearned premiums on all outstanding risks... 114,986.29
Due for commission and brokerage............. 9,040.82
All other liabilities............................ 12,619.58
    Total liabilities....................$164,746.34
Total premiums in force December 31, 1908.....$144,205.62

BUSINESS IN OREGON FOR THE YEAR

Claims Allowed.

Robt-Trousor, Sup'r dist 15 $52.00
W. Orton, Sup'r dist 15, 2500
B. W. Hays, et al. dist 2. 340.85
"$275.85 on special fund and $57.50 from general fund."
Geo. Hodges, powder for county. 15.80
P. A Babcock, work on Rock Creek road, 8.00
E. M. Standon, Sup'r dist 8. 43.75
Wm. Sharp, work on dist 9, 262.90
"$169.15 on special fund and $93.75 on general fund."
R. R. Guynn, work on dist 5, 91.50
F. M. Terman, work on district 20, 258.00
L. C. Norton, work in dist 15, 58.25
John Kentta, supplies purchase for county. 827.84
Austin Rosebrook, care for Lou Hall. 24.90
R. N. Warnock, for team and saddle hire. 5.00
Newton & Nye, supplies. 29.00
Hart & Wood, lumber. 16.67
Toledo Dray Co., supplies, 6.60
T. M. Seits, money paid on grader. 75.00
Albert Martin, building crowder dist 15. 15.00
Ted McElwain, team work. 2.00
R. S. VanCleve, supplies for Owens. 16.30
Hall Brothers, supplies. 2.20

more work in that district during its present year, unless, in case of necessity."
John C, Dougherty, dist 3, 289.75
A, B, Hunt. Sup'r district 11.49.00
Irwin & Hudson, supplies, 53.55
A, L, McDonald, work in district 14, 129.60
Benton County care of prisoner 7.00
F W Carson, work on road, 3.75
Frank Burkel, bread for Owen 2.55
Newport Signel, printing, 5.40
E I Williamson, Sup'r dist 19, 395.85
Bushong & Co, supplies, 279.80
Lula Miller, refund of taxes, 25.15
Chandler & Houser, et al, supplies, 6.06
F W Carson, work for surveyor, 3.00
Gust Olson, draying, 11.50
J P Robertson, work in dist 6 194.00
Ross E Moores & Co, supply's 17.65
R W Henry, et al cost bill in state vs Perry Wheeler, 12.35
Z M Derrich, et al surveying on Olala road, 98.50
" " " Newport Silitz road, 31.00
" " " Beaver Creek road 121.00
" " " Big Elk road 75.00
M Wygant, et al surveying Newport Slitz road, 43.25
Cowing & Cowing, supplies, 13.70
Robert Trousor, work on road 43.05
A L Porter, surveying Olala

Yaquina Bay, photographed when the bay was at an extreme low tide on a summer day in 1912. The city of Newport is in the center of the photo. The Yaquina Bay lighthouse can faintly be seen on top of the bluff overlooking the entrance to the bay. Below the bluff, the ocean breakers roll over the entrance to Yaquina Bay as it flows into the Pacific Ocean. The waterway opening on the left is King's Slough, and the land extending out into the bay on the left is Idaho Point. This area was in the center of an unbroken Indian reservation extending along the coast for a distance of 125 miles. During the latter part of 1865, Congress opened for settlement a strip of land through this tract. This entire area has been the heart of the coast Indian reservation since the 1850s, made up of twenty-four tribes which moved into this area as wards of the government.

The Oregon Pacific daily passenger train arrives in Yaquina City on August 12, 1887, bringing participants to the first meeting of the Oregon Press Association. The call for this meeting went out from J.R.N. Bell of the *Roseburg Review*, Collins Van Cleve of the *Yaquina Post*, and Martin Luther Pipes of the *Corvallis Benton Leader*. Pipes was elected the first president of the association, with Jess M. Shepherd from Albany and Robert J. Hendricks of Salem as vice presidents, and Charles Nickell from Jacksonville as secretary. Dean Eric W. Allen from the school of journalism at the University of Oregon commented in one of his lectures, "The Portland press was poorly represented at the Yaquina City meeting, as they felt this small city had ambitions of wrestling the leadership of the Pacific Northwest away from Portland."

The front page of an 1883 issue of the *Yaquina Post* when Collins Van Cleve was owner and publisher. Van Cleve was a "one-man Chamber of Commerce" working to build and sell Yaquina City. He also served as the first "collector" for the newly built U.S. Custom House at Yaquina city, one of the first on the Pacific Coast.

The Yaquina Hotel was built by the Oregon Pacific Railroad in 1885. It was a three-story frame structure with sixty rooms, and a block-long wooden sidewalk built on stilts connecting the hotel with the railroad station. The hotel was built to accommodate patrons who had used the railroad from Portland and valley points to Yaquina city, and would be continuing their trip to California via the ocean liners owned by the railroad. Railroad mishaps, poor handling, and loss of their ships resulted in almost total failure for the Oregon Pacific Railroad. This eventually resulted in the railroad being taken over by the Southern Pacific. The hotel was dismantled in about 1910, with some of the lumber used to build the new Abbey Hotel in Newport.

The Yaquina railroad station in 1912 with the arrival of the daily passenger train pulled by SP 2085 (4-6-0 Schenectady). In the foreground are the homes of Dell Bohananas and Sydney Pruetts along with the Ira Branch Grocery Store. Across the bay is West Yaquina school and the homes of A.W. Wright and Judge D.P. Blue.

The Oregon Pacific's six-stall roundhouse, with their No. 7 (a 4-4-0 Cooke built in 1886) on the hand-operated wooden turntable. The small, fifty-six ton locomotive is being made ready for the daily trip into the valley. Note the oceanliner at the wharf *(extreme left)*. Charles Schmidt's small boathouse, seen beside the tracks, was the town of Yaquina's only saloon. The railroad management would not permit liquor to be sold on the mainland. Some of the passengers crossing the bay from Newport to board the train felt that a "short-snort" conditioned them for the train ride ahead.

Inside the Oregon Pacific Railroad's machine shop in Yaquina in 1890 before the building was dismantled and moved to Albany. Some of the men shown are: I.T. Hulme, Master Mechanic *(extreme left)*; others are Fred Simmons, Walter Smith, F.M. Stansell and R.A. Stratford.

The town of Toledo is located on an arm of Yaquina Bay roughly nine miles from the ocean. This is a photo from 1915 looking west down Main Street. The railroad tracks and old Toledo were on Waterfront Street *(left)* with the railroad station in the center of the street. The buildings on Waterfront Street were the oldest in the town and were all destroyed by fire on July 13, 1937. Some of these included: the Pacific Hotel owned by L.M. Adams; C.M. Duncan Plumbing Shop; Toledo Cleaners; Thatcher's Barber Shop; and Atwood Shoe Shop. The railroad station was made of brick brought in on an ocean-going vessel to Yaquina City, then transported by rail to Toledo. The public spirited people of Toledo built the station for the railroad. It was torn down a few years ago to make way for a through truck route.

The Yaquina City football team in 1908 ready for the big game against Toledo with the railroad tracks and the town of Toledo in the background. The team was made up entirely of railroad employees or relatives of railroad personnel. They are *(no particular order)*: Gus Ridgeway, fireman; Lloyd Pruett, son of a section foreman; Charleton A. Bump, railroad mail clerk; William C. Hoeflein, conductor; Paul Tollefson, son of a bridge carpenter; Adlia J. Casteel, son of a locomotive engineer; Claude Jones, son of an express messenger; Harry Devilbliss, news agent; Ira Branch, railroad mail clerk; Frank C. Barnes, warehouse assistant; and "Kraty" Cronise, brakeman, team captain and former player for Oregon Agriculture College (now Oregon State University).

LINCOLN COUNTY SENTINEL

VOL. I.   TOLEDO, OREGON, FRIDAY, DEC. 6, 1912.   NO. 28

DIRECTORY.

COUNTY OFFICERS.

Judge,   Chas. H. Gardner,
Sheriff,   Bert Geer.
Clerk,   R. H. Howell.
Treasurer,   G. B. McCluskey.
W. E. Ball,   Assessor.
Superintendent,   R. P. Goin,
Surveyor,   Z. M. Derrick,
Coroner,   Dr. F. M. Carter,
Commissioners,   John Kentta,
Claus Luderman.

CITY OF TOLEDO.

Mayor,   I. R. Wishart,
Recorder,   F. N. Hayden.
Treasurer,   Sam Center.
Marshal,   A. M. Gildersleeve.
Councilmen:— J. J. Gaither,
George Hoglein, C. P. Merrell, H.
F. Nulton, C. W. Davies and A.
T. Peterson.

CHURCHES.

METHODIST EPISCOPAL

Sunday School   -   10:00 a.m.
Preaching at   -   11:00 a.m.
Preaching at   -   7:30 p.m.
Prayer Meeting every
Thursday evening at 7:30 p.m.
Ladies' Aid Society meets every
second and fourth Tuesdays in
each month.
Rev. F. S. Clemo, Pastor.

Society.

A. F. and A. M.—Lincoln Lodge
No. 124. Stated communications,
second Monday in each month at
8 o'clock P. M.
W. E. Ball, W. M.
R. P. Goin, Sec.

I. O. O. F.—Toledo lodge No.
108; meets every Wednesday eve.
Visiting brothers, always welcome.
A. H. Weber, N. G.
Carl Gildersleeve, Sec.

W.O.W. —Pocahots Camp, No.
999. meets at Woodman Hall

OBITUARY.

Samuel Kirkwood Booth, was
born in Jasper co. Iowa, Sept.
5th. 1860; and died at Toledo,
Oregon, Nov. 29th, 1912. Age
52 years 2 months 24 days. He
was married on April 27th 1882
to Miss Sarah C. Shaffer, at Altoona, Iowa. To this union nine
children were born, three of whom
dying in infancy, or early childhood.
The six living to mourn
the loss of a loving father are
Mrs. Anna Ports, of Florence,
Oklahoma, Mrs. Dolly Skallerud,
and Miss Jennie Booth of Portland Oregon, Joel, Mable, and
Loren of Toledo. He also leaves
a widow, Mrs. Sarah C. Booth
two brothers and two sisters,
Dr. W. H. Booth of Los Angeles,
Calif., Mrs. Eliza Westfall, Mrs.
Luvena Learn, and Dr. J. E.
Booth, all of Lebanon, Ore.
Mr. Booth has also left behind
many friends in Toledo, and in
Douglas Co. and elsewhere.
In February 1902 he with his
family united with the First
Presbyterian Church at Pond
Creek Oklahoma, and with this
religious organization he remained a member till death. He also
took pleasure in fraternal societies, being a member of A.F.A.M.,
I.O.O.F., and Modern Woodman
of America. The funeral services were held on Dec. 2, 1912, in
the M. E. Church at Toledo Ore.,
Rev. F. S. Clemo preaching the
sermod. At the ceramony the
Masons had charge, and the
beautiful and impressive order of
service was used. The day was
rainy and disagreable, but a large
concourse of friends attended the
services thus. showing their re-

OFFICIAL DIRECTORY.

LINCOLN COUNTY

Joint Senator .... G. S. Wright
Joint Representative .... J. S. Cooper
Judge .... C. M. Brown
Sheriff .... J. H. Ross
Clerk .... Ira Wade
Treasurer .... J. L. Hyde
Commissioners {George King
                    {F. A. Thompson
School Superintendent ...... George Bethers
Assessor .... J. H. Lutz
Surveyor .... M. Wygant
Coroner .... W. W. Soule

TOLEDO CITY

Mayor .... H. W. Vincent
Aldermen {Chas. Gardner
            {Geo. L. McCaulou
            {T. P. Fish
            {R. S. Van Cleve
            {M. N. Anderson
            {R. A. Arnold
Marshal .... J. A. Hall
Recorder .... Otto O. Krogstad
Treasurer .... G. L. Gray

SCHOOLS

TOLEDO PUBLIC SCHOOLS, WORK INcludes the 9th grade.
Prof. O. B. DeLaurier, Principal.
J. F. Stewart, } Directors.
J. B. Crosno, }
O. E. Bacus, }
C. E. Hawkins, Clerk.

CHURCHES

ST. JOHN'S CHURCH, EPISCOPAL, SERvices, Third Sunday of each month at 11
o'clock a. m. and 7:30 p. m.
Rev. Frank Jones, Minister in charge.

METHODIST EPISCOPAL CHURCH, SERvices every Sunday at 11 o'clock a. m. and
8 p. m. Sunday School 10 a. m. Prayer
meeting Thursday evening at 8 p. m.
Rev. C. M. Braas, Pastor in charge.

UNITED EVANGELICAL LUTHERAN,
Services in the Norwegian language every
fifth Sunday. Services in English at 8
o'clock p. m. same day.
J. C. Reinertson, of Silverton.
Pastor in charge.

COUNTY NEWS

NEWPORT

Judge Cake and wife of Portland
Oregon is spending a few days at
Oregon's most popular resort for
the benefit of Mrs. Cakes health.

Capt. McJunkin of the launch
Toledo came down Monday with a
number of Toledo people among
them we noticed were Sheriff Ross,
John Olstedahl, Geo. McCaulou, Geo.
King, Henry Howell and others.
These gentlemen came down to
make some arrangments for the
funeral of Allen Parker, who died at
his home in Toledo on the 31st inst.,
from old age and infirmitives.
Mr. Parker was one of the pioneers
of Oregon and well and favorable
known throughout the state.

F. H. McDonald is moving his
store building on his lots in the
north end of town. Capt., Tom has
charge of the work.

P. M. Abbey is cleaning and fitting
up his hotel and annexes with paint,
paper and a new linalum carpet on
the dinner room floor. Every thing
will be as neat as a pin.

Capt Jacobson is also cleaning,
papering and renovating the Bay
View so as to accommodate the
many tourist and visitors that will
come here this summer.

The Ocean House, the oldest house
in the town is being repaired with
a new foundation and a new coat of
paint. This hotel has the distinction of having the finest location in
town. It commands a magnificent
view of the bay, ocean and surrounding country. Mrs. Case is the owner
any proprietor.

The Bayley house will be fitted up

under supervision of Miss Alexander
of Toledo; No. 55. has secured the
service of Miss Edith Miller of Sodaville. Miss Miller comes to us very
highly accomended from Linn county
where she has had six years experience teaching in the public schools.
Miss Alexander is well known in
Toledo. She will make her home
while teaching with Mr. and Mrs.
M. W. Randal.

The officers of district 55 has been
working on their schoolhouse. They
expect to have a neat, commodious
house when completed.

A few Drift Creek people, who
are ardent devotees of the dance, attended the hop on Big Elk last Friday night April 28.

M. W. Randal and C. L. Knapp
went to Toledo Friday 28, inst.,
with a four horse rig expecting to
bring out our "school marm's" but
Mr. Randal was disspointed or else
was fearfully of trusting the life of
their teacher to the reckless driving
of Knapp at least he did'nt get her
and expects to have to sent for her
again. Miss Miller arrived all right
rather badly shaken up however.

SILETZ

We have had very fine weather
and everybody enjoys the weather.

April 23, Easter Sunday, was a
very happy day with the Christian
people. Both churches were crowded.
About 2 o'clock in the afternoon
plenty of egg shells could be found in
the groves and on the banks of the
river.

A game of base ball was played
on the 22, which was very swift,
that is, the ball went swift but not
the players. A game was played on

The oldest settlement within the confines of the present Lincoln County is Elk City, located at the head of navigation on Yaquina Bay, eight miles east of Toledo. In June, 1873, the Corvallis & Yaquina Bay Wagon Road Company built a warehouse at the western end of the recently completed toll road between Corvallis and Elk City. The Yaquina River flowed into Yaquina Bay and was used to handle the traffic of passengers and U.S. Mail beyond Elk City to the coast. The small settlement as seen in 1900 shows the Yaquina River and the two hotels built in the 1870s. The Elk City Hotel *(center)* was managed by W.T. Bryon, and the Elk City House *(only portion of roof showing)* was managed by James E. Dixon. In front of the hotel is the I.O.O.F. (Odd Fellows) also housing the Masonic Lodge. Notice the community church with the steeple in the background.

Elk City is a sleepy little village today. The country store *(left)* is the center of activity and is owned by Sharron Stopyak. There are a few remaining homes along with the one hundred-foot covered bridge *(right)* built in 1924. The fishermen in the area enjoy the Yaquina River. A daily freight train passes through Elk City on its way to and from Toledo. The highway was built in 1922 but it misses this town completely.

Morrison is some twenty miles from the Pacific Ocean and has an interesting history. The area was named after Barney Morrison, a man from Tennessee who had homesteaded the area. In 1900, the post office requested the town name be changed from Morrison to Pioneer. The change was made officially at the post office, but the townspeople and the railroad continued using the original name. This photo of Barney Morrison and his wife, Jimia Stover Morrison, was taken on April 1, 1907, in front of the railroad station/post office as they celebrated their sixty-first wedding anniversary. It was a gathering of sons and daughters and their families. Shown are: Ruth A. Embrees, Chester and James Morrison, Tabitha Simpson and Josephine Bevins. Barney died later the same year on September 18, 1907.

LINN COUNTY

The Albany railroad station built in the 1880s was a combination ticket office and hotel dining room, a necessary accommodation as the railroad did not carry diners at that time. This photo was taken in 1902 after the Southern Pacific secured ownership of the Oregon & California Railroad. Meal service was handled by J.A Gross who can be seen standing under the station canopy. Train operations were handled by the agent, William Blair Rice *(extreme right)*. The locomotive is O & C No. 5, a 4-6-0 Baldwin built in 1870. This photo was taken during the noon hour as rail patrons were inside having lunch. The train came through Albany daily, making a twenty minute stop for lunch.

The stern-wheeler *Pomona* passes through the opened Oregon Pacific Railroad Bridge in about 1905, heading towards Portland. Built in 1898, the *Pomona* was 134 feet long and could carry seventy-five tons of freight and only drew thirty inches of water. The swivel-span structure was constructed in 1887 over the Willamette River at Albany and was at that time the longest wooden drawbridge in the world.

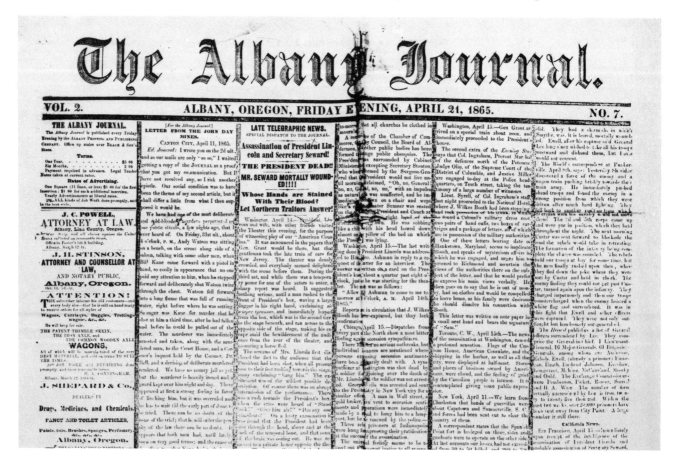

DAILY ALBANY HERALD.

VOL. I.—NO. 170.   ALBANY, OREGON : FRIDAY MORNING, JULY 9. 1886.   15 CENTS A WEEK

LATEST DISPATCHES.

Dempsey Knocked Out.

San Francisco, July 7.—Jack Dempsey arrived this morning on the State of California, completely knocked out by sea sickness. He says he threw up fifteen pounds of bile He registered at the Baldwin Hotel.

Caught Kidnapping.

San Francisco, July 7.—A Chinaman named Ah Sam, formerly employed as a house servant by C. W. Horn, at 609 Brush street, visited the house last night and made an attempt to kidnap Jimmy Horn, the four-year-old son of his former employer. Sam was arrested and taken to prison.

Fast Trains of the Northern.

Helena, July 7.—President Harris, of the Northern Pacific in an interview having his attention called to the item that fast passenger trains would be put on the Union Pacific next month, said the Northern Pacific would meet any time the Union Pacific would make from common points between Chicago and Umatilla.

Sherman in San Francisco.

San Francisco, July 7.—General Sherman arrived here to attend the coming encampment. He will take a good rest, going to various parts of the state. Last night he visited the George Thomas Post, G. A. R. The general, in a fine speech, eulogized Lincoln as the greatest man that ever lived. He said: "while the great statesmen and great generals surrounded him on all sides he towered like a giant above them all."

Turning the Tables On Us.

London, Ont, July 7.—A great sensation was caused here to-day by the announcement of the flight to the United States of Edward Harris, member of a prominent firm of solicitors, besides taking $20,000 in cash. Various funds belonging to wealthy clients are in a serious state of entanglement. The total loss is not known but it is ———

OLYMPIC GARDENS.

The Mounted Sword Contest a Draw—Other Events.

Portland News:

Nearly 1,000 people were present at the opening of the new Olympic gardens last evening. In the early part of the evening there was a display of fireworks followed by athletic exercises.

The first event was a foot race fifty yards, best two in three, heats. Ben Hirsch, Fred T. Merrill and Wilson entered. Hirsch won the first two heats, and Wilson second, Merrill third. Time 5¾ seconds, 5¼ seconds.

The event that excited the most interest was the mounted sword contest between Maroney and Whalen. They were clad in armor made of steel wire and presented a formidable appearance as they rode around the arena preparatory to fighting. A. G. White was chosen referee and the men were sent to their corners and told to remain their until the cornet sounded. In the first attack Whalen got one point without much trouble, and Maroney one in the second equally as easy. The men came together with a rush for the third attack and parried for a while. Maroney getting one point. In the fourth attack Maroney gained one point, but received two blows in return on his back that cut into the skin. The fifth attack was the most spirited of all, and the men went at it with a will. Whalen made three points and Maroney two. The fight was declared a draw, although Maroney had five points and Whalen four.

William Grant, F. T. Merrill and Murray entered in the half mile running race. Merrill won first prize, $10, and Grant, second, $5, Murray distance.

The Bob-Eared Cayuse.

From the Heppner Gazette:

The cayuse is a bird who is constantly making himself felt as a part of the ———

DAILY ALBANY DEMOCRAT.

VOL. 2.   ALBANY, TUESDAY MORNING, JULY 18, 1876.   NO. 186.

ALBANY DEMOCRAT

ISSUED DAILY (SUNDAY EXCEPTED) BY

MART. V. BROWN,

PUBLISHER AND PROPRIETOR.

OFFICE.

In Democrat Building, corner of Second and Broadalbin street.

Terms of Subscription:

One Year (by mail) $6 00
Per Week (served by carrier) 25

BY TELEGRAPH.

Eastern.

Washington, July 14.—The sundry civil appropriation bill, as it passed the House, originally appropriated $14,857,000; in its passage through the Senate $15,150,900 was added in the bill. As agreed upon by the conference committee, the Senate recedes from its former views to the amount of $412,500, and the House recedes and allows to be added to the bill the sum of $350,000, making the appropriation in the bill about $15,950,000.

The Sun's Washington special says President Grant was prostrated yesterday by the heat, and his physician has ordered him to take a recess.

The Tribune's Washington special says that the President, one day last week, gave audience to an Ohio private citizen, one in no way connected with public life, and voluntarily talked with him on the political situation. Among other things, the President criticised very severely Hayes' letter, and thought it reflected on the administration. He further said of the gentlemen: "I hope the time will come when the American people will be permitted to elect their President for as good a time as they choose." The President's entire manner indicated complete dissatisfaction with the political situation and much personal anger. The feeling is growing that the President has cut loose from his party affiliations, and is reckless of its official acts on the party in the future. Indeed, he says he don't intend to be governed by advice of Republican Senators, but have his friend around him. If he pardons the whisky thieves already convicted, as it is feared he probably will, the Republican journals and organs will openly disavow him and show he was disavowed at the close of his term.

By Atlantic Cable.

London, July 13.—The court circular says that at a banquet given by Sir Salon Jung a few days ago, he proposed the health of the Empress of India. One distinguished member of the House of Commons, said to be John Bright, abstained from responding, while other guests simply drank to the Queen. It is said that the Prince of Wales, who was present, has since asked for an explanation of the occurrence.

Pacific Coast.

Eureka, July 15.—It is rumored that the Richmond Mining Co. will suspend operations on the first of August. The great decline in silver is assigned as the cause of the suspension. Part of the management are inclined to continue active operations, provided all the men in the employ of the company would stand a reduction of 50 cents a day each on their wages, while the present low figures for silver shall rule, with the understanding that the price of labor should be advanced to the old rate whenever the silver market will warrant the change. It is hardly probable however, that such an arrangement could be effected with the miners, for the reasons they well understand the difficulty of getting the wages advanced when once cut down.

C. W. VOLLUM,

BOOK BINDER

PAPER RULER,

Blank Book

Manufacturer,

BOOK, CARD AND

Job Printer.

No. 5 Washington street

PORTLAND.

Blank Books made to desired pattern. Newspapers, magazines, music, etc., bound in any style with durableness and durability.

All of the buildings on this street in the small community of Halsey were built in 1904 or 1905, as the original structures were all destroyed by fire in 1903. The buildings in this 1910 photo *(left to right)*: Roma V. McCully General Merchandise Store, with the I.O.O.F. (Odd Fellows) lodge room upstairs; The Bert Clark Confectionery; The M.V. Koontz General Merchandise Store, owned by Martin Van Buren Koontz; The Halsey State Bank, where Clyde Harry Koontz was president; Marks & Walton Drug Store, owned by Timothy I. Marks and Levi E. Walton; and the last store is believed to have been the Fischer Lumber Company, where C.J. White was manager.

AGRICULTURE
HORTICULTURE
LIVESTOCK

Halsey Enterprise

DAIRYING
WOOL, MOHAIR
POULTRY

Established in 1912. Vol. 16. No. 44. Halsey, Oregon, Thursday March 8, 1928. Devoted to the Interests of Halsey and Linn County

Spoon River Sparks

(By an Enterprise Reporter)

J. N. Elliott and family spent Sunday at O. J. Albertson's

Mrs. A. L. Falk and daughters and son were business visitors in Brownsville Saturday.

W. A. Falk and family were transacting business in Albany Saturday.

The members of the Pollyanna cooking club and the Bachelor boys sewing club postponed their meeting until next Friday so that they could attend the club moving pictures at the Halsey school house.

Mrs. William Ralston and children, Donald and Elsie, and Mrs. Russell Chin of Oregon City visited at the H. L. Straley home one evening last week.

Mrs. Merwyn VanNice and children and the Misses Grace Kirk, Doris Howard and Nellie Falk were among those who attended the Freshmen Glee club concert at Salem.

Louise Seefeld and her guest, Margaret Halsey, were guests at the Henry Seefeld home Saturday night and Sunday.

Edna Falk has returned to her home after spending the past two weeks at the C. L. Falk, Sr. home while Ava Falk has been assisting Mrs. Gillette, who has been on the sick list, with her house work.

Mrs. R. E. Bierley and son Kenneth and Mrs. Fred Falk and daughter Delma spent the week end at the Theodore Falk home in Salem.

SCHOOL NOTES

Edited By Wilma Wahl

Dr. Allen of the University of Oregon favored the school with a number of pictures on club work last Friday evening. Owing to a broken spring in the machine not all the pictures were shown. Several of the outlying district schools were present.

Retta Armstrong has been helping Mrs. Coleman by teaching the 4th grade long division.

Cyrus McCallister has been absent the last two days and has left school for good.

Wanda Veatch was absent Monday.

Kenneth Workinger was absent Wednesday and Thursday of last week and Inez Miller was absent all last week.

There was no program this week and the student body met and heard the report of Bessie Reynolds and Francis Leeper who were delegates to Corvallis.

The Junior program last Wednesday was as follows:
Reading "Flintigan on the Farm" by Frances Norton.
Vocal solo, "What Does It Matter" Jennie Nicewood.
Vocal solo, "Among My Souvenirs" "All for My Baby" and "Happiness" by Keith Hayes.
Reading, "My Dogs" by Jennie Nicewood.
Dialogue, "Two of a Kind."

This week the high school is enjoying examination.

Things That Can't Be Explained

JIM—PLEASE EXPLAIN THIS BURN IN MY NEW TABLECLOTH

HALSEY AND VICINITY BREVITIES

Hill & Company unloaded a car of John Deere tractors the first of the week. The tractor is becoming a necessary factor on the farm and sales are growing.

The work of rebuilding the Third street telephone line is nearly completed and greatly improves the appearance of that thoroughfare. The telephone service has been greatly improved since repair work began.

Mrs. William Curtis and son Dale of Lebanon spent Monday afternoon and night at the home of their daughter and sister, Mrs. ...

... Grove last Saturday. Mr. Veatch will remain at the farm for a few days.

The Charity Grange literary society are putting on a play at the grange hall next Saturday evening. The play is "Beads On a String."

Mr. and Mrs. Clark Chastain and three children spent Sunday at the home of Mrs. Chastain's parents, Mr. and Mrs. Fruit.

Tuesday afternoon Mrs. Buford Morris and little son drove to Albany and visited friends and relatives. They returned home with Mr. Morris after the meeting of ...

Shedd Personals

(By an Enterprise Reporter)

Mrs. C. C. Dickson had her tonsils removed last week at the Corvallis general hospital, and has been suffering hemorrhages of the throat.

Mrs. Vernetta Cox of Portland spent Friday visiting her sister-in-law, Mrs. L. R. Wilson of Shedd.

Mr. and Mrs. L. Zimmerman transacted business in Albany Saturday.

The junior class of Shedd high school served a hot lunch to the school children to raise money for the junior-senior banquet.

Mr. and Mrs. Harry Poland, accompanied by Otis Farwell and Lillian Miller were visitors in Portland Sunday.

Mr. and Mrs. Harry Springer and daughters, Ardis and Lois, were guests at the John Swatzka home in Tangent Sunday.

Mr. and Mrs. George Chandler of Pine Grove were Shedd visitors Sunday.

A road meeting regarding the new market road east of Shedd was held at Albany at the court house Saturday.

Fayetteville Items

(By Special Correspondent)

The members of women's missionary society tendered a surprise party and handkerchief shower to Miss Tempa Jean Brock at her beautiful country home east of ...

Peoria News Items

Mr. and Mrs. George Bayne and son John attended a birthday dinner at the home of their daughter and sister, Mrs. George Workinger near Halsey Sunday.

M. C. Hughes of Alpine, former Peoria barber, was a business visitor here Saturday.

Mrs. Fay Githens and George Githens attended the community program at Oakville Friday.

Peter Freerkson was a business visitor in Peoria Monday.

Mrs. Mary Porter and Mrs. Dale Forbes visited Mrs. Porter's mother, Mrs. Alice Dunn, Saturday.

Rev. Metcalf was looking after business transactions in Corvallis Monday.

Mr. and Mrs. J. S. Lamar have been having some improvements made in their home, Lester Miller of Fayetteville is doing the work.

Mrs. Anna Githens and Lola Shaw were Albany visitors Monday.

Fred Gujon of Brownsville was visiting relatives in Peoria last week and while here pruned fruit trees for J. S., J. W., and W. B. Lamar.

Wayne Mode and Thomas Logan were visitors to Cottage Grove last Monday.

Little Betty Taylor eldest daughter of Mr. and Mrs. Percy Taylor, had the misfortune to fall from the porch at their home Monday afternoon and was hurt quite bad, but later was reported to be resting easy.

Mr. and Mrs. J. S. Lamar and Miss Lida Gregory of Shedd were ...

THE WEEKLY NEWS.

Independent In All Things, Neutral In Nothing---Fearless And Free

Vol. 4, No. 23 HALSEY, OREGON, FRIDAY APRIL 20, 1894 $1.50 Per Year

BOOK OF CHRONICLES.

CHAPTER XII.

Now there dwelt in and about Halsey a remnant of a sect calling themselves Prohibitionists, chief among whom were Barton the Bell wether, Elias the Bunch Grasser, Sanderman the Virtuous and Stevenson the Righteous.

Now these Prohibis are a peculiar people. They fain would compel other people to do even as they do—to drink as they drink, to be the same in their uprisings and down-sittings. Verily they are the salt of the earth, and no other name is given under heaven whereby men might be saved than that of Prohibitionists. Their Golden Rule is: "Compel all others to do even as we do."

Now Barton the Bell-wether spake to several Republicans, saying: "Verily, McFeron is a good man for sheriff. He is a Christian and his name is an offense to the nostrils of the whisky men. Behold, I am for McFeron, and for Flem Smith and for Rutherford. And there be other Prohi's like me, and we shall go to Albany and will have our convention to endorse them and thereby will we make our votes count for men of our principles, for otherwise will our votes be the same as if given to a whisky man." And one Davis, who wanted to be county clerk, spake unto McCulloch the Sleek-tongued saying: "I will vote for McFeron if you nominate him." And again he told him as he started to the convention of the Self Righteous, "I will be as good as my ... will see if his word be ...

... nation."

Now at their meeting at the City Hall, Sanderman the Virtuous arose and said: "Men and brethren, look upon me! Behold the lamb that was tempted but would not be led astray. I can't be bought. Verily, the Republicans tried to seduce me but I laughed them to scorn. I took their money but in a few days I returned it with virtuous indignation. Verily, we are not for sale at those figures. We will never vote our principles if it puts every saloon keeper in office in the land. Behold, I have preached temperance and union to you ever since my arrival here. Verily, I am your Moses. If you will join with me and vote as I do you shall escape the fires of damnation. Let us be one." And all the Prohis said Amen.

Now great is the merriment of the people thereat.

Deafness Cannot be Cured

by local applications, as they cannot reach the diseased portion of the ear. There is only one way to cure Deafness, and that is by constitutional remedies. Deafness is caused by an inflamed condition of the mucous lining of the Eustachian Tube. When this tube gets inflamed you have a rumbling sound or imperfect hearing, and when it is entirely closed Deafness is the result, and unless the inflamation can be taken out and this tube restored to its normal condition hearing will be destroyed forever; nine cases out of ten are destroyed by catarrh which is nothing but an inflamed condition of the mucous surfaces.

We will give one hundred Dollars for ...

OAKVILLE.

J. W. Barton was in town last week. Come again, J. W.!

Mr. Johnson Wh... son, of Portland, are visiting fr... here.

J. C. Brown, can... for representative on the prohib... ticket, was in town last week. J... all right.

Our Postmaster is busy fixing his lot, and planting out flowers and fruit trees. He has the nicest c... lot in town.

Rev. Acheson, ...nford, J. E. Hamilton and H... in went to Albany Saturda... prohibition convention.

The political pot ...ng high here. Four parties are al... in the field and another is forming. There is one thing we can't understand ... why it is that Oakville is not better represented on the tickets. There are plenty of good men here to fill all the offices ...m governor down to coroner, and as fo... intellect, we have more of that than anything else. We have men that would accept a nomination on any ticket, a... can talk high tariff one day and free tra... the next; can talk prohibition three hundred and sixty four days and vote with a party that has saloon keepers on its ticket.

DAISY.

To the Public.

We have this day sold the business formerly conducted by ..., under the name of the Oriental Tea Company to Messrs. Pitner, Umstead & Smith, who will hereafter conduct the business at the old stand ...

BRIEFLY STATED.

Subscribe.

Dr. Micheher has a new hat.

Here's the place for job printing.

For lagrippe use Dr. Shoop's cure.

Douglas Taylor was in Portland last week.

J. L. McCulloch took a trip to Albany Tuesday.

Frank Bayne, of Peoria, was in town last Sunday.

Sheriff Jackson was up from Albany this week.

J. W. Senft, of Albany, was in town Thursday.

Will & Stark, the leading Jewelers Albany Oregon.

Mr. Joseph Tyler, of Salem, has been in Halsey this week.

Miss Allie Wilson is teaching school in the Lobster country.

M. Senders, of Albany, was doing business in Halsey this week.

Every bottle of Dr. Shoop's Catarrh Cure is warranted.

Mexican Silver Stove Polish causes no dust. Ask Stafford, Garrett & Co.

Dave Bond and wife came from Prineville last week and are visiting here.

Ask Stafford, Garrett & Co. for Mexican Silver Stove Polish. No dust.

For rheumatism use Dr. Shoop's cure. Every bottle warranted.

Messrs. J. E. Cross and Daniel Standish visited in Brownsville last Sunday ...

Beautiful weather, this.

Cleve Pearl drove to Brownsville Tuesday.

F. M. French, the leading Jeweler, Albany.

Look out for some new ads. in this paper soon.

John Gates of Harrisburg, was in Halsey Sunday.

Use Dr. Shoop's cough cure; guaranteed.

Halsey is now already for a seige of good weather.

Attorney Kelly, of Albany, was in Halsey last week.

Mr. and Mrs. J. T. Smith were in Albany this week.

Taylor Bros. shipped a carload of sheep to Portland last night.

Just received at J. E. Cross': a fine lot of bird cages.

George Stainburn, of Cottage Grove, was in Halsey this week.

Mrs. Jessie Sullivan, of Harrisburg, was in town Wednesday.

Mrs. H. G. Plymate went to Eugene yesterday where she will visit.

Jeweler McCulloch is now spending his spare hours riding a bicycle.

Mr. Morris Merrick is visiting in the country this week with Chas. Gibson.

Mrs. L. Walton returned from Eastern Oregon Sunday, where she has been visiting.

C. F. Wright, the Harrisburg furniture man and undertaker, was in Halsey last Tuesday.

The small farming town of Scio in Linn County was quite proud of its girls' ball team in 1910, seen here at the city fair. They are *(left to right, back row)*: Ollie McDonald; Emma Cain; Agnes Wesley; Roger Cain, coach; Agnes Cain; Vella Brenner; and Bess Morris. *(From left to right, front row)*: Edwin Holland, teenage boy wearing a dress; Birdella Brenner; and Lucy Wesley.

Faculty members of Mineral Springs College, a small Presbyterian college at Sodaville in May, 1898, enjoy a relaxing period on campus: *(left to right)*: Ethel Maria Starr (Mack), Stella Parrish, Dr. Herschel Leroy Mack, and Lucy Newland.

FACULTY.

L. R. BOND, D. D., President of College.

F. E. MORTON, A. B.—
    Science and Greek.

H. L. MACK, B. E. L.—
    Mathematics and General History.

J. H. BOND, Student in Classical Course—
    First Year Latin, Algebra, Physical Geography.

ETHEL M. STARR, B. E. L.—
    English Literature, Rhetoric, Drawing.

I. G. McCULLY, Master of Accounts—
    Principal of Business Department.

LOUISE NEWLAND, Bachelor of Accounts—
    Typewriting and Shorthand.

LUCY NEWLAND, B. E. L.—
    Principal Preparatory Department.

J. HOUSER, B. E. L.—
    Arithmetic, Physiology, History.

Mrs. L. D. BECK—
    Vocal and Instrumental Music.

Mineral Springs College.

Courses:— Classical, Scientific, Literary, Normal, Business, Musical and Theological.

Sodaville, Or., ..., *1899.*

MALHEUR COUNTY

The small farming community of Nyssa is well-known for raising sugar beets. This 1915 photo shows unpaved Main Street, looking west. The buildings are *(left to right)*: Nyssa Drug Store, L. Spiers Clothing, Masonic Temple, a theater with the marque reading "Moving pictures tonight 15 cents and 10 cents," Nyssa Confectionery, Golden Rule Store, Brunswick Billiard Hall, H.M. Housh Grocery, and at the far end of the street is the Methodist Church. Some of Nyssa's leading citizens of the day shown here are: Louis Spier, clothing store owner; J.C. Himber, grocer; C.G. Forbes, owner of the Star Hotel; Edward H. Super, hardware store; C.C. Wilson, lawyer; N.J. Minton, manager of the Bank of Nyssa; J. Boydell, owner of the Boydell Mercantile; and H.T. Francis, manager of Empire Lumber Company.

This small farm house in Malheur County in 1912 features "drop siding" on the outside and a fancy glass door, along with a picket fence, giving this home class distinction. Notice the "kick plate" at the bottom of the gate to prevent loosening of the pickets by "in a hurry" users and the long johns on the clothesline.

MARION COUNTY

A 1916 photo of the Cherry Blossom Parade in Salem shows Queen Estella Wilson and her maid, Rosalie Bach, with Frank George Deckelbach, the "King Bing." The royal consort is riding in the back seat of a new, light six 1916 Studebaker, surrounded by members of the Cherrians. This organization, started in 1913, paraded the Salem streets in their white uniforms every year during cherry blossom time. They advertised the beauty and enjoyment the white hills and valleys offered to everyone as the cherries came into bloom.

This 1900 photo shows the end of the car line at 12th & Howard streets in Salem. The home belonged to the grand old man of Willamette University, Professor James Thomas Matthews, who for many years was head of the Mathematics Department. His two sons shown here are: Donald Navarre Matthews (with hat) and Oliver Vincent Matthews. This small electric street car was originally a horse-drawn car, converted into an electric car in about 1898. The house was torn down in 1955.

Salem as it looked in the late 1860s or early 1870s. This photo is of the south side of the unpaved State street between Liberty and Commercial. It was probably taken by W.P. Johnson, one of Salem's early photographers (notice his sign in the background). The buildings are *(left to right):* Tioga block, now in the Capitol Tower building; the bookstore and photographic gallery of Wiley Kenyon (Salem's first mayor); the Thomas McFadden Patton building; and on the corner, the Ladd & Bush bank. The concord coach *(center)* may have been used in the Portland-California stage service before the coming of the railroad.

Hundreds of locals in 1902 came to honor Salem's Spanish-American war veterans returning from the Philippines. The train was pulled by locomotive SP-1764, a new 2-6-0 woodburner just received from the Baldwin Locomotive works in Philadelphia. The roof of the Salem railroad station and one of the city street cars can be seen in the background.

In 1913 Salem was a rapidly growing city. Besides being the capitol of the state, it had become the second largest city, population-wise, passing Astoria for the honors. The photographer has captured this shot of the busiest corner in the city, that of Commercial and State Streets. The Salem Heights car, #54, built in St. Louis, Missouri in 1893, heads north on Commercial Street, while car #73, built in Danville, Illinois in 1910, runs east on State Street. To the far right is a portion of the Ladd & Bush bank, built in 1869. The Dearborn building, second from the corner with three large upstairs windows (occupied by Snider Printing Company at the time), is the oldest building on this block. It was built in 1868.

THE OREGON VIDETTE.

VOL. 7—NO. 6. SALEM, OREGON, THURSDAY, DECEMBER 16, 1886. NEW SERIE

A SPLENDID STORY.

FETTERS OF GOLD!

A ROMANCE OF REAL LIFE!

....BY ROBERT LINCOLN....

CHAPTER II.

HERE this singular young lady broke off abruptly, and for some few moments paced the tesselated floor of the conservatory. She approached the door, and paused there a second, evidently to ascertain if anyone was moving.

Then approaching Gerald, she laid her white jeweled hand on his arm, and looking earnestly into his pale face, she said:

"Gerald, when in Italy you told me that you loved me, you offered me your hand and I accepted you. I do not know whether it is right to say so, but Heaven knows that I love you—oh, yes, I love you with all my heart and soul! I love you now, though your love fled long, long ago. The love I have for you still remains firmly rooted in my heart, and will so remain until the grave shuts me out of sight forever! Gerald—Gerald." she said pleadingly, "do not turn from me like that! Think of what my sufferings have been since you so suddenly departed, and without one kindly word."

"Miss Compton," replied Gerald, gravely,, "have you not asked yourself the question as to why I so suddenly departed?"

No answer.

"This was the reason," continued Gerald; "and no doubt you know of it. You were introduced to me as a lady moving in the best society, and for a long time I knew you as such. I fell in love with you, and I certainly loved you with as pure and as honest a love as man ever had. I proposed and you accepted. The time passed on. I, young and inexperienced, got mixed up with a set that frequented gambling-dens. I was tempted ... between them.

At last Miss Compton said;

"Clara, you have guessed the result of this interview?"

"I have,' was the low reply.

"He is engaged.'

"Engaged?"

"Yes; to his cousin. Engaged to his cousin, and until he told me, I did not know it, Yet, I thought I was kept well informed in regard to his movements."

"Pardon me, Miss Compton; did you ask Mr. Kingslake why he did not inform you of Mr. Lethbridge's engagement?"

"Oh, yes, I asked him that and a lot more ere he left the house. He tells me he knew absolutely nothing about it. He says that Mr. Lethbridge is very reserved in all matters respecting his family and relatives.'

"Well, Miss Compton, Mr. Lethbridge certainly does not deserve the great affection you have ever had for him. So far as I can see his love was not for you, but for your money.'

"No—no, Clara; do not say that. I believe his explanation as to why he so suddenly left Italy, and I curse the hour when, for the first time in my life, I sat down at a gambling table. Oh, why—why did I ever do such a thing? For a number of years my mother kept the gamester's house; for years and years I was associated with those who patronized her house. I saw them play; but I never played myself—never, until he came to Italy. And, after all, he is another's! But it shall not be! it shall not be! To be his wife was the height of my ambition. Why, I know not, except that I have loved him almost from the first ... tell her that the unlucky instrument had been unfairly treated.

Like most young ladies, Miss Clissot had a lover, and he, as a matter of course was the guest of the evening whenever Miss Clissot gave an At Home.

His name was Henri Istram, and he was a tall, but somewhat thin, and moreover a somewhat peculiar-looking man of about thirty.

His business was that of a 'merchant in the city,' but then so many people so describe themselves.

No one thought of asking in what particular or peculiar class of goods he dealt.

Clara had first met him at Brighton and the intimacy had continued in London.

Now, the day after the affair in Wigmore street, Clara received a lawyer's letter.

Imagine her astonishment, her great joy, when the letter informed her that she was an heiress.

(TO BE CONTINUED.)

Humors of Law-Making.

(New Princeton Review.)

A certain member of the New York assembly, when the roll was called on a bill, asked the clerk for a "detailed statement of the count." Another member spoke thus of a bill: "Mr. Speaker, this is a party bill, and I ask my party friends to stand by me and help me to pass it." On another occasion, when the assembly showed signs of weariness, he announced: "Mr. Speaker, I will now withdraw all my further remarks on this bill." A third member commenced to speak against a bill affecting some of his property: "Mr. Speaker, I arose in a quasi capacity." Here a colleague pulled his coat-tail. The member shook him off, and began again: "I arose in a quasi capacity." Again came a jerk at his coat-tail, and in a hoarse whisper, the colleague was heard to say: "Whisht? come off wid yer Greek." Still another member delivered himself thus on the question of contract labor in the State prisons: "This is the vital cobra of destruction that is stamping out the lives of workingmen in this State."

On one occasion a pugnacious member of the majority listened as long as he could to the attack of a minority member from his party, and then broke out with ...

THE WHOLE TRUTH.

Answer to the Statement made by the Bolting Democrats---Authorized Statement.

To the Democracy of the City of Salem and Marion County—Gentlemen:—Certain persons styling themselves members of the regular Democratic party of the City of Salem a few days ago published a statement of their grievances in the Daily Statesman which was false and untrue in every particular. The members of the regular Democratic City Central Committee have up to the present time refrained from answering these alleged grievances for the reason that as true and tried Democrats they desired the election of the regular Democratic city ticket and did not wish to do or say anything that would tend in the least to the defeat of the excellent ticket placed before the people of Salem for their suffrages, or the demoralization of the Democratic party of the city. The bolting Democrats make a statement to the effect that there was a call made in 1884 for Democratic primaries and city convention and at that time a chairman of the city central committee was selected, as well as committeemen from the different wards and that no other primaries or convention was held for that purpose since that time. The truth is that a call was issued prior to December 4' 1885, for the holding of city primaries on December 4, 1885, and city convention for December 6, 1885. At the city convention T. L. Golden was elected as chairman of the city central committee. At the primaries so held committeemen were selected from the different wards.

The cause of the apparent trouble that has arisen is that T. L. Golden, who was a member of the citizens' committee of twenty-five, had determined on the advice of others, among the number W. T. Gray, a member of said committee, and F. N. Gilbert, not to issue a call to nominate a Democratic ticket, but to prevent at all hazards the call being made, and nominate in place of a Democratic ticket, what should be called a citizens' ticket, composed of Republicans and Democrats, Golden and clique were ready and willing to throttle the party organization.

Before the call was issued a number of democrats went to Golden (who was recognized as the legally constituted ... to issue a call for Tuesday evening for city primaries (the same evening that the regular democracy were to hold their city convention). The regular democracy, knowing full well that there were not to exceed ten to fifteen men who were in sympathy with the Golden clique (and four of those candidates for postmaster of our city), resolved to attend their primaries for the purpose of clearly showing to the people that the claims of Golden and advisers of having the support of the united democracy was untrue. In the first ward the regular democracy elected the entire list of delegates that had been selected on the preceeding Saturday; the third and fourth wards did the same. In these three wards there was not a dissenting vote. W. J. Herren, who was chairman of the meeting which was held at Gilbert Bro's office (with closed doors) was present at the meeting in the first ward, and stated publicly that he approved of all that had been done there. The second ward was the only one in which there was any trouble. Although Golden and his followers were outnumbered five to one, as chairman of the ward meeting he refused to decide questions determined against him, although outvoted in every instance. He had no right to usurp the power and authority that did not belong to him, H. D. Boon being the proper person to call the meeting to order. Further, the meeting was called to order fifteen minutes earlier than advertised. Finding that they had been outvoted in all the wards, Golden and his advisers (not to exceed five, all told), met in secret conclave at Gilbert Bros' office and selected persons, a part of whom they knew would not act with them, as delegates from different wards (without any meeting in the wards). They issued a call for a meeting of delegates that they had selected, to be held at Gilbert Bros' office (with closed doors), and that no one but the delegates so selected should be admitted to the meeting—not even a reporter. At that meeting nine of the twelve delegates selected were present, several of whom assured your committee that they attended to prevent the nomination of a separate ticket, and as mere lookers-on, and not for the purpose of approving of the proceedings. At this meeting a set of resolutions was adopted, and it was determined that no ticket should be nominated, but that the citi... but too true in the case of the parties last above named. Either rule or ruin is their motto. In this case political ruin they certainly have brought upon themselves. They have been tested and found wanting.

W. E. McAFEE,
Chairman Democratic City Central Committee, Member State Central Committee for Marion County.
B. N. HAYDEN,
E. J. HUMASON,
J. G. FONTAINE,
Democratic City Central Committee.

DEGRADED AMERICAN LABOR

The Republican Party the Pioneer in Legislation Against the Workingmen

(Indianapolis Leader.)

It is a curious fact not generally known that the first and only law ever passed by Congress expressly authorizing the importation of foreigners under the contract to perform labor for a stated time in place of our American workingmen, was put through the two houses when the Republicans had an overwhelming majority in each. It is true, also that the record fails to disclose any opposition to that atrocious measure on the part of Republicans in either house. Its champion in the Senate was the Hon. John Sherman, of Ohio, and in the House, the Hon. E. B. Washburne, of Illinois.

The bill is entitled "An act to Encourage Immigration." It passed both Houses July 2, 1864, on a conference report signed by Sherman and Anthony on the part of the Senate, and by Washburne and Windom on the part of the House, and it was approved by the President July 4, 1864, which was the last day of the session.

The managers of the bill exhibited hot impatience to put it through before the close of the session. June the 28, on motion of Mr. Sherman, "all prior orders" of the Senate were postponed, and the bill was taken up and passed, the ground of haste, being as stated by the Ohio Senator, that "wages were very high" in this country, and we needed importation on that account. In the House Thad Stevens had moved to go into Committee of the whole on one of the great appropriation bills, but withdrew his motion on Washburne's earn...

SCIENTIFIC MISCELLANY.

Random Notes of Importance and Significance.

FROM A DECADE'S HISTORY.

(Written for the OREGON VIDETTE.
BY E. S. CHADBOURN.

ANTIQUITY OF AGRICULTURE.

According to De Candolle, agriculture came originally, at least so far as the principal species are concerned, from three great regions—China, the southwest of Asia (with Egypt), and intertropical America. Drawings of figs in the pyramid of Gizeh furnish an example of the cultivated plants of Egypt at a period perhaps 4,000 years ago, when the people had already made some progress in civilization, and must have had an established agriculture—several centuries old at least. In China the cultivation of plants must date from an equally early period, for in 2700 B. C., the Emperor instituted an annual ceremony of planting rice, sweet potato, wheat and two kinds of millet. In America, agriculture is perhaps not quite so ancient as in Asia and Egypt, if we are to judge from the civilization of Mexico and Peru, which does not date even from the first centuries of the Christian era. However, the widespread cultivation of certain plants, such as maize, tobacco and the sweet potato, argues a considerable antiquity, perhaps 2000 years or therabouts.

CHANGES IN ENGLAND'S COAST LINE.

In a recent address to the British Geologist' Association. Mr. W. Topley stated that the land-area of England is probably as great as 500 years ago, although certain coasts have been much worn by the waves. On the coast of Holderness and Norfolk the sea is gaining on the land at the average rate of from two to three yards a year, while during exceptional gales, the loss in places has been many yards in a single day. The eroded material is deposited elsewhere, as in the estuaries of the Humber and the Wash, forming new land quite equal in extent to that carried away.

HAIR.

Muschenbroeck found that a human hair, fifty-seven times thicker than a silkworms' thread, would support a weight ... called ferments, which also cause br... to rise. From this point of view t... are profitable in industry and comme... But, in addition to these useful microb... there are others which are injuriou... us. Such are the microbes that prod... diseases in wine, most of the change... alimentary and industrial substan... and, finally, a large number of the ... eases to which men and domestic anim... are subject. The germs of these diseas... which are only the spores or seeds... these microbes, float in the air we brea... and in the water we drink, and t... penetrate to our bodies' interior. Th... is not a single day, nor a single insta... in which we cannot be said to be in c... tact with microbes, which are, in f... the invisible agents of life and death.

FIRE-PROOF RUBBER.

A new compound of caoutchouc, which the name of "woodite" is sugg... ed, has been produced by Mrs. A. Wood, an English lady. The substa... possesses the elasticity of indiarub... undergoes no change by exposure, an... claimed to be absolutely uninflamma... It is proposed to use it for covering unarmored parts of war-ships and to... boats.

GRAPE SEEDS.

French horticulturist, Mons. Nol... has found that the seeds of the fi... varities of grapes germinate more quic... than those of the common sorts, and t... seeds fresh from the fruit germinate b... ter than those which have been dried.

Pen Paralysis.

Pen paralysis, sometimes called writer's cramp, is the cramping or we... ening of the muscles of the fingers a... forearm in such a manner as to ren... them more or less uncontrollable by t... writer, and may result from one or m... of several causes, namely: From writi... constantly and rapidly on the finger mo... ment, with the finger in a cramped po... tion; from the use of a small and high... polished holder which necessitates a ti... grip upon it, thus unduly compressi... the musles in the parts touching the hol... er, also subjecting all the muscles of t... fingers to a constant strain; or the mu... cles may be so over worked from lo... continued and hurried writing that th... break down from sheer exhaustion. ... from the latter cause, the only remedy ...

SALEM DAILY RECORD.

VOL. 1. SALEM, OREGON, TUESDAY EVENING, NOVEMBER 3, 1874. NO. 171.

SALEM DAILY RECORD.

S. A. CLARKE, Publisher.

PUBLISHED EVERY EVENING, EXCEPT SUNDAYS.

Subscription price, 25 cents per week.

TELEGRAPHIC.

EASTERN.

NEW ORLEANS, Nov. 2.—The election promises to be quiet. Up to this hour (1 P. M.) no disturbances of any kind is reported. Persons fraudulently registered are challenged by either party and not allowed to vote. Many negroes vote the Conservative ticket. Dispatches from Franklin and N. Iperia say everything is quiet. In the latter parish negroes are reported as voting strongly with the whites. Up to this time everything is peaceable.

CHICAGO, Nov. 2.—An *Inter-Ocean* Washington special says enough is known of the character of the annual estimates to show that they will be more than ten millions less than for last year. Estimates, both for public works under the Engineer's bureau and those under the Treasury are very much reduced. The cost of the navy remains about the same, while the army in some of its supplies, was cut below its real necessities at the last session of Congress. Secretary Belknap has regulated his estimates strictly in accordance with the law. The Treasury estimates have been based exactly on what the House gave in its last appropriation. The cost of the Indian service will not be diminished. The deficiency in the Postoffice Department will be increased, owing to the rapid extension of added facilities of the Department. As a total result, however, the reductions are something over $10,000,000.

The public debt statement shows a reduction of $681,434 during October. Currency balance on hand, $16,396,770.

The Secretary of the Treasury has issued a call for $500,000 of coupon bonds, 5 20's, to be redeemed February 3d, at which date the interest will cease.

The Postoffice Department has made a contract, by telegraph, with L. M. Starr to continue the Puget Sound mail service between Olympia and Victoria, twice weekly, until next January, when the contract awarded on Saturday commences.

General Humphreys, in his annual report, asks for the following, among other appropriations for the Pacific Coast, for the year ending June, 1875: For fort at Fort Point, $50,000; fort at Lime Point, $50.000; fort at Alcatraz Island, $50,000. No appropriations are asked for battries at Point San Jose, Angel Island, Fort San Diego, or for the removal of Rincon Rock. An appropriation of 20,000 is asked for defences at the mouth ...

BRITISH COLUMBIA.

Ex-Mayor Harris was knocked down by a cart at Victoria, last week, and sustained a fracture of the small bone of the right leg.

The steamer Los Angeles took to San Francisco from Victoria last week the following amounts: Bank British North America, $60,-234; Bank British Columbia, $56,040; F. Garesche, $14,670. In all, $131,744.

The contract for building the penitentiary at New Westminster has been let to Kinsman & Styles of Victoria, with whom are associated Muirhead & Mann, carpenters; A. & W. Wilson, plumbers; and Conn. Mitchell, painter. The contract price is $139,365. Work will be commenced as soon as possible.

Starr Bros. of the Puget Sound Mail Steamship line have leased that portion of the water front extending from Broderick's wharf to the Hudson Bay Co.'s wharf at Victoria, for a term of ten years, and will immediately proceed to the construction of a first-class wharf for the use of their steamers and shipping.

The farmers on Fifteen Mile creek, Wasco county, are requested to meet at Beezley's school house, on Saturday, the 17th of November, at 11 o'clock, for the purpose of organizing a joint stock company to build and operate a grist mill.

There has not been a marriage in Baker county for three months.

Advertisers, Take Notice.

The weekly circulation of the WILLAMETTE FARMER is 2,250—that of the *Statesman*, 720.

The *Statesman* "claims" a daily circulation of 600, while ours is 576—but the combined circulation of the RECORD and WILLAMETTE FARMER is MORE THAN DOUBLE THAT OF THE DAILY AND WEEKLY *Statesman*.

This fact the advertising public should not fail to notice and appreciate.

Indigestion's Martyrs.

Half the diseases of the human family spring from a disordered stomach, and may be prevented by invigorating and toning that abused and neglected organ with Hostetter's Stomach Bitters. Let it be borne in mind that the liver, the kidneys, the intestines, the muscles, the ligaments, the bones, the nerves, the integuments, are all renewed and nourished by the blood, and that the digestive organs are the grand alembic in which the materials of the vital fluid ...

Oregon State Fair, 1874.

FIRST PREMIUM

WHEAT-CLEANER.

The Oregon Granger.

INVENTED BY SAMUEL DAW, BENTON CO., Oregon, and patented Nov. 25, 1873, received the prize as the

Best Wheat Cleaner

Ever made in the State.

Price, - - - $30.

I shall immediately commence the manufacture of this machine at Salem and Corvallis. J. W. LEAVITT, agent at Salem; BALDWIN & CO. at Corvallis Or address me at Corvallis. [oc3tf] SAMUEL DAW.

LUCIUS BELL,
Successor to J. M. KEELER & Co.,
95 Liberty st., - - NEW YORK.
Commission Agent

FOR BUYING AND FORWARDING FROM New York via Isthmus, Pacific Railroad, and Cape Horn, all kinds of Merchandise, and for the sale of Products from the Pacific coast, for the collection of money, &c. oc18tf

MARBLE WORKS.

MONROE & STAIGER,

Dealers in

Monuments,

....AND....

Head and Foot Stones.

ALSO,

MANTELS,

..AND..

Furniture Marble to Order

ADDRESS,

A. J. MONROE, Salem, Oregon. | WM. STAIGER, Albany, Oregon.

may9tf

Best Chance

..TO..

INSURE

AGAINST

W. WEATHERFORD. J. W. WEATHERFORD.

WEATHERFORD & Co.,

Wholesale and Retail Dealers in

DRUGS, PAINTS,

OILS, GLASS,

Patent Medicines.

CHEMICALS,

Perfumery

TOILET GOODS,

Etc., etc.

PURE WINES and LIQUORS,

For Medicinal purposes.

Medicines Compounded, and Prescriptions Filled.

Weatherford & Co.,

May 6-y Commercial street, SALEM.

E. D. WILLIAMS,

(Successor to Mercury Office,)

BOOK & JOB

HERMAN & HIRSCH,

GRISWOLD'S BLOCK, SALEM.

OFFER TO THE

CITY & COUNTRY TRADE

An immense stock of Goods to be sold at

GREAT BARGAINS

FOR CASH IN HAND.

Heavy Stock of Everything

HEAVY STOCK OF

Brown and Bleached Cottons,
Sheetings, Shirtings, Checks,
Denims, Stripes, Etc., Etc.

HEAVY STOCK OF

Ladies' Dress Goods, (best class and newest styles)
Poplins, Pongee Silks, Diagonals,
Japanese Silks, Alpaccas,
Merinos, Cashmeres,
Delaines, Worsted Goods.

HEAVY STOCK OF

Fancy Goods of all kinds,
Ribbons, Buttons, Etc., Etc.

HEAVY STOCK OF

Ladies' and Children's Shawls,
Reversible Ottoman Shawls,
Camel's Hair Shawls,
Plaid Wool Shawls.

HEAVY STOCK OF

Ladies' and Children's Felt Skirts,
And other Balmorals,
Ladies' Underwear.

HEAVY STOCK OF

Gentlemen's and Boys Underwear,
Men's and Boy's Clothing ...

DAILY EVENING MERCURY.

Vol. II.   SALEM, TUESDAY EVENING, DECEMBER 19, 1876.   No. 79.

The Oregon Arena.

VOL. I.   SALEM, OREGON, MONDAY, OCTOBER 24, 1864.   NO. 15.

THE WEEKLY TALK.

VOL. 6. SALEM. OREGON, THURSDAY, MAY 13, 1886. NO. 2

WEEKLY TALK,

SUBSCRIPTIONS.

One year	$1 50
Six months	1 75
Three months	1 00

S AT REPUBLICA T CKET

For Congressman: Binger Hermann, of Douglass county.
Supreme Judge J. B. Waldo of Multnomah.
Governor, T. R. Cornelius, of Washington,
Secretary of State, Geo. W. McBride, of Columbia.
Treasurer, H. L. Marston, of Umatilla.
Sup. Public Instruction, E. B. McElroy of Benton.
State Printer, F. C. Baker, of Multnomah.
First Judicial District—For Judge, L. R. Webster; Prosecuting Attorney, H. Kelly.
Second—For Judge, R. S. Bean; Prosecuting Attorney, T. W. Rayburn,
Third—For Judge, R. P. Boise; Prosecuting Attorney, C. A. Johns,
Fourth—For Judge, L. B. Stearns Prosecuting Attorney, Henry E. McGinn.
Fifth—For Judge, Frank J. Taylor; Prosecuting Attorney, T. A. McBride.
Sixth—For Judge, M. L. Olmstead; Prosecuting Attorney, Geo. O. Holman.
Seventh—For Judge, George Watkins; Prosecuting Attorney, Wm. R. Ellis.

MARION COUNTY REPUBLICAN TICKET.

For State Senators.
J. B. DIMICK, M. L. CHAMBERLIN
J. B. LOONEY,
For Representatives.
J. T. GREGG, C. F. HICKS,
D. J. PENDLETON,
W. B. CULVER, SAMUEL LAYMAN
A. M. LAFOLLETT.
For County Judge.
T. C. SHAW,
For Commissioners.
G. P. TERRELL, J. N. DAVIS,
For Clerk.
M. N. CHAPMAN.
For Sheriff.
JOHN W. MINTO,
For Treasurer.
AUG. GIESY,
For School Superintendent.
GEO. A. PEEBLES,
For Assessor.
BENTON PATTON,
For Surveyor.
JOHN NEWSOME,
For Coroner.
W. C. WARINNER,

Flashes by Telegraph.

Philadelphia, May 6.—There was intense excitement here yesterday among idle workmen over the news of the riots and bloodshed in the western cities, which they received with silence. There is much speculation as to whether the tradesmen now out on a strike in this city would resort to force. Over ten thousand men are idle. Over forty two employers have signed pledging themselves to require their men to work ten hours a day, or to close their establishments.

Milwaukee, May 6.—All is quiet in the city this morning. Troops continue to guard the threatened establishments at Bay View and the South Side. No riotous assemblage has been reported thus far this morning. The trouble is believed to be over.

Albany, New York, May 6.—In the assembly Chamber to-day, after a long political debate, an appropriation of $200,000 was made to improve the Erie Canal.

A resolution was adopted requesting Congress to pass a bill for the relief of Colonel J. D. Stevenson, of San Francisco, 86 years of age, a veteran of the war of 1812 and of the Mexican war, and who took the first regiment of Mexican volunteers to California.

Two bills were introduced declaring boycotting not to be a conspiracy or misdemeanor under the law.

Chicago, May 6.—There is a greater feeling of confidence apparent this morning in the ability of the authorities to preserve peace. The outlook continues threatening in certain quarters and the police expect they may be called upon to disperse gatherings in certain portions of the city. But the arrest of a few Anarchists yesterday insured a feeling that this element will no longer prove troublesome, in view of the fact that the police now believe all the leading instigators of the recent trouble have been caged, with possibly a notable exception. Collecting evidence against the conspirators is proceeding rapidly. In the vicinity of the nests of the Anarchists, in the southwestern portion of the city, large detachments of the police, heavily armed continue to patrol the streets. The report that the lumber men propose to start their mills to-morrow is without foundation, as they are bound by a cast iron contract to grant no concessions whatever. Threats continue to be made to burn the immense mills and lumber yards, but every precaution is taken to prevent this.

New York, May 6.—Services at Grant's tomb on Decoration Day will be international in their character, St. Johns, N. B., will send a floral piece; Hamilton, Bermuda, will send two living palm trees; the Minister from Mexico will see that his country is represented. General Williams, of Havana, writes that the Governor-General will direct that the Island of Cuba will also be represented. All the states and territories will send flowers, and many will be represented by delegates. General versed the decision. Morrow since has strenuously striven to have the first decision of Brewster approved by Attorney General Garland, and to-day received a communication from Garland in which Brewster's first decision was affirmed.

San Francisco, May 9.—Investigation of the House of Correction is revealing a horrible state of affairs. It has already placed Superintendent Sedgwick in the light of a brutal demon. The Examiner boldly accuses him of murder, and cites two cases where death resulted derectly from his inhuman treatment. Conningham, an old man, was beaten and choked insensible by the guard, and then while on the filthy floor, was drenched with many buckets of water. After this, by order of Sedgwich, he was thrown into a scalding tub. When taken out large patches of flesh adhered to the tub. He began to sink, and soon died. The other case was nearly equal.

Denver, May 9.—Captain Lawton of the Fourth Cavalry, is in command of the combined forces in the field and is moving south on the trail of the hostiles, whom it is reported are making for the mountains. Hohnstadt, of Sonora, reports that Chief Magnus is killed, and claims to have possession of his scalp. General Miles declares that a vigorus campaign will be carried on until every hostile is killed or captured.

Vienna, May 9.—Both Turkey and Greece are rapidly massing troops on the frontier and are hurrying forward reinforcements and reserves. An engagement may be looked for at any moment.

Chicago, May 10.—The day freight handlers' strike is virtually at an end. Every freight depot in the city was in active operation to-day, partly with new and partly with old employes. The roads have made no concessions whatever, and refuse to treat with committees from the strikers but have restored to their places such of their old employes as they have vacancies for. The companies are now able to handle freight with their former rapidily, and everything is running as before.

All the mental works, with one or two exceptions, commenced operations to-day, with about half the average force.

Chicago, May 10.—When the mob of Anarchists which wrecked Rosenfeld's drug store last Wednesday, and had mashed everything except the bottles containing liquids, they turned on them and commenced gulping down their contents without further inquiry. The labels on the bottles were Greek to the ignorant crazy mob, which was bent on having a gratuitous drunk. Since that time it has been learned that many rioters have died from the effects of poisoning, and that scores of ... the main track. The freight train was running at the rate of thirty miles an hour and came along at midnight and crashed into the obstruction before the engineer had time to reverse. The conductor, Thomas Connors, and engineer, Thomas Momsil, the fireman, Michael My..., were killed instantantly.

Evansville, May 11.—Early this evening a terriffic wind and rain storm struck this city, tearing off the roofs of houses, breaking windows, terring tress up by their roots and doing other damage. No loss of life has been reported. The estimated loss of property is $300,000.

Washington, May 12.—In the Senate to-day Senator Mitchell submitted a concurrent resolution expressing it to be the sense of Congress that negotiatsons should **be entered into between the United States and the Chinese government with a view** to securing such modification of the present treaty with China as would result in stopping the coming of Chinese to this country except diplomats and their servants; and except also in the case of persons at sea, driven to seek a place of shelter. The concurrent resolution was referred to the Committee on Foreign relations.

Joliet, May 12.—A most destructive cyclone swept over Odell, a small village forty miles south of here, on the Chicago and Alton road, this afternoon. A passenger train arrived here this evening, and the passengers state that the cyclone approached as the tarin was nearing Odell. At first they saw the roof of the elevator rise and sail off and then the collapse of the elevator building; next a hotel fell and a small house was raised high up in the air and tumbled over like, as though it was constructed of so many feathers, and then it shattered in a thousand pieces. The tornado was blowing parallel with the track, otherwise the train would have shared the fate of the buildings. The train resumed its journey without giving its passengers time to asertain the number of casualties, but they are reported to be large.

Later details from Odell state that the cyclone did an enormous amount of damage, injuring many and one probably fatally. There is hardly a building in the town but what has suffered from the storm.

Joliet, May 12.—A fearful storm struck Joliet at 8 o'clock this evening. A deluge of rain and hail inundated the earth while thunderbolts were deafening, and the electric display was unparalleled. Robinson's circus was showing here at the time. In the midst of the performance the storm struck the tent, completely wrecking it. Women screamed, and the animals raced and roared, causing a regular stampede amid the sheets of glaring lightening, the dranching rain, the awful peals of thunder and the resistless gale. Three persons

Races at Walla Walla.

The eleventh annual exhibiton of the Washington Territory Agricultural and Mechanical Association will be held at Walla Walla September 6th, 7th, 8th, 9th, 10th and 11th 1886. The following is the programme of the races:

Monday—First Day—Purse $200; running; 600 yards, Derby stakes, running; for three-year olds, $50 each, half forfeit $300 added; one mile and a half. Purse $200; trotting; 3:00 class.

Tuesday—Second Day—Pioneer stakes; running for the two-year olds $50 each, half forfeit, $300 added; five-eights of a a mile. Purse $500; one mile dash. Washington Territory stakes trotting; for four-year olds and under, $50 each half forfeit, $300 added.

Wednesday—Third Day—Purse $300; one-half mile dash. Purse $500; trotting 2:25 class.

Thursday—Fourth Day—Purse $300; running for two-year olds, handicap; one-half mile. Walla Walla stakes; trotting; for two-year olds, $50 each, half forfeit, $250 added; mile heats.

Friday—Fifth Day—Citizens Purse; running free for all; one and five-eights of a mile. Society stakes; trotting for three-year olds and under, $50 each half forfeit, $200 added.

Saturday—Sixth Day—Purse $300; running; three-fourths of a mile. Purse $250; trotting; 2:40 class. Citizens Purse $700; trotting free to all. Parties intending to be present at the meeting and desiring stalls for their horses are requested to write to the Secretary in advance, stating what horses they have and what stalls they are likely to require.

The Associstion reserves the right to alter, amend or postpone any or all of these races should the Board of Directors in their judgement and for cause deem it expedient so to do.

A Boy Without a Country.

(Washington Letter to the Chicago News.)

Some years ago Charles Busch, a naturalized German-American, accompanied by his pretty Italian wife, sailed for France to accept an engagement as tenor singer in one of the opera companies in Paris. En route a child, who was named Charles Herman Busch, was born to them. The mother

What Became of the Clay Eater of Rocky Gulch.

It was the fall of 1885, and our company had made quite a success. We had in our employ four miners from the Pennsylvania coal mines, one coal oil refiner, and a man from North Carolina, known as the "North Carolina Clay Eater.

About the time we were to close work for the winter, one of my partners said, he guessed we had better pay off our men and quit work. He took the men however and went to the mine as usual, but returned in the afternoon and informed us that the mine had caved in and killed all the men. We had however our suspicion, that he had planned the cave in, in order to save the three thousand dollars we owed them, but we knew it would not be safe to express such an opinion. The next day however we went to work to recover our tools, and when we unearthed the men the thought occurred to me that the coal miners would make good fuel, as they looked dingy as though their bodies were thoroughly impregnated with coal. So I rolled them all down the hill to the cabin and threw all of them but the oil refiner on the fire. I took him and crammed an old rope in his mouth and set him up in one corner of the cabin for a lamp, using the rope for a wick, and he made a splendid light. The men I threw on to the fire burned briskly, all but the "clay eater" he soon looked like a piece of crockery. After he had been on the fire about three weeks, I took him out and carted him off, and was as solid and as polished as a stone jar. My intention was to make a whiskey cask out of him, so I took him up and shook the cinders out of him, corked him up and stood him close to the lamp, split the sole of a shoe and stuck it in his mouth for a funnel, then I took the whiskey barrel and emptied the contents into him, and he held nearly the whole barrel.

Things went on all right till near spring when one night my partners got into a drunken row, knocked over the "clay eater" who in his fall upset the "Pennsylvania" lamp which exploded setting the cabin on fire, and in the confusion which ensued I took the dust and fled. When the miners returned in the spring to resume work the burnt remains of eight men were found on the spot where the cabin stood, which the miners supposed had been surprised and destroyed by the Indians. So ends my story of the "Clay eater of the Rocky Gulch."

ROCKY MOUNTAIN JIM.

A Monster Petition.

The Anti-Chinese petition which was circulated so extenisvely in this city and State by the Knights of Labor, says the San Francisco Alta of a late date, has been closed up and transmitted to Washington. Wells, Fargo & Co. exibited a patriotic

Whispers in the Air.

MR. EDITOR:

As there seems to be so much in the air at this time of the year—all kinds of miasma, contagious diseases incident to youth and elderly persons also.—I am induced to send you a few words as to the alarmingly prevalent complaint, viz.: prohibition. I am very old fashioned, very; and cannot endure the idea of any religious college taking part in political issues. It will not be wise for any minister to run for any position in the present divided state of things. And young theologians will be much disturbed in their course of study if they presume to mingle politics and religion. It cannot be done without more or less of misunderstanding, and many obscure words which will hinder instead of help to remove the barriers. Too many women are saying their say about these things, and it never will do, for women do quarrel fearfully when once they begin. And they are apt to get excited; men never do—good, sensible men, and no others ever take part in politics. I have been loth to speak, but now I see so many cogitations, so many fierce-looking men sittiug on the fence, watching for something, I'm concerned for the peace and welfare of the quieter portion of the population—the women. I believe in personal liberty. And it will be a very great infringment upon this liberty if a few men overturn the liquor traffic when it is so well protected by the laws of the United States. We hope this will be well considered by all political aspirants and the lookers on. As clubs seem to be the order of the times we would ask: will our reform clubs consider the propriety of removing from their rooms the pool and billiard tables, and the smoking rooms? Our young men, whose mothers are teaching them to avoid dangerous ground, and whose constant prayer is that they will keep a clean record, so that they may become useful and Christain citizens, cannot visit such places with safety. Are smoking, billiards and pool rooms, component parts of true reformation? Is the gospel temperance standard to be lowered to meet those "who have not been educated beyond that point," the pool table? Let all temperance workers have a clean record, for we want all Oregon for God and purity. Our young men are the hope of the nation, and if they will take heed to the way in which they begin public public life—or life in its real meaning, the hearts of those who knew them in childhood and boyhood can safely trust in them. As they advance they will realize better what this trusting means.

ON DUTY.

American Unionist.

VOL. 3. SALEM, OREGON, SATURDAY, JULY 17, 1869. NO. 48.

Weekly American Unionist

ISSUED EVERY SATURDAY.

HUNTINGTON & CO., Publishers.

THE OFFICIAL PAPER OF OREGON AND U. S. OFFICIAL PAPER.

TERMS OF SUBSCRIPTION.—For one year, in advance three dollars. For six months, in advance two dollars.

Remittances may be made by mail, at the risk of the publisher, if mailed in the presence of the Postmaster.

☞ Office in Stewart ...ick Building, Up Stairs

Stimulant.

George D. Prentice has been a constant drinker for forty years. For ten years he has been a drinker of the lignum vitæ order. Here is a temperance lecture by him—worth a score, at least, of the Good Templar exhortations and misrepresentations:

"There are times when the pulse lies low in the bosom and beats low in the veins; when the spirit sleeps, which, apparently knows no waking, sleeps in its house of clay, and the windows are shut, the doors hung in the invisible crape of melancholy; when we wish the golden sunshine pitchy darkness and wish to fancy clouds where no clouds be. This is a state of sickness when physic may be thrown to the dogs, for we wish none of it. What shall raise the spirit? What shall make the heart beat music again, and the pulses through all the myriads thronged halls in the house of life? What shall make the sun kiss the eastern hills again for us with all his old awakening gladness, and the night overflow with moon-light, love and flowers? Love itself is the greatest stimulant, the most intoxicating of all, and performs all these miracles, and is a miracle itself and is not at the drug store

Gough's Apostrophe to Cold Water.

The celebrated apostrophe to cold water given in one of Gough's temperance lectures, is a gem. Pouring out a glass of water and advancing toward his audience, and lifting it above his head, he said:

"Look at that ye thirsty sons of earth! Behold it! see its purity! How it glitters as if a mass of liquid gems! It is a beverage that was brewed by the hand of the Almighty himself! Not in the simmering still, or smoking fires, choked with poisonous gasses and surrounded by the stench of sickening odors and rank corruption, does our Father in Heaven prepare the precious essence of life—the pure cold water, but in the green glade and grassy dell, where the deer wanders and the child loves to play; there God brews it; and down in the deepest valley where fountains murmur and the rills sing, and high upon the mountain tops where the storm clouds brood and the thunders crash; and away far out on the wild sea, where the hurricane howls music, and the big waves roll the chorus, sweeping the march of God—there he brews it—that beverage of health giving water, and everywhere it is a thing of beauty, glimmering in the Summer rain, shining in the ice gem—till the trees all seemed turned into living jewels, spreading a golden veil over the setting sun, or a gauze around the midnight moon; sporting in the cataract, sleeping in the glaziers, dancing in the hail showers, folding its soft curtain softly about the windy world, and weaving the many clouded iris that is erpha's zone of the sky, whose woof is the sunbeam of Heaven, all checkered over with celestial flowers by the mystic hand of reflection, still always is it beautiful, that blessed

A Pithy Sermon to Young Men.

You are the architects of your own fortunes. Rely upon your own strength of body and soul. Take for your motto, self-reliance, honesty and industry; for your star, faith, perseverance and pluck, and inscribe on your banner, "Be just and fear not." Don't take too much advice; keep at the helm and steer your own ship. Strike out. Think well of yourself. Fire above the mark you intend to hit. Assume your position. Don't practice excessive humility; you can't get above level—water don't run up hill—put potatoes in a cart over a rough road and the small ones will go to the bottom. Energy, invincible determination, with a right motive, are the levers that rule the world. The great art of commanding is to take a fair share of the work. Civility costs nothing and buys everything. Don't drink; don't smoke, don't swear; don't gamble, don't steal; don't deceive; don't tattle. Be polite; be generous; be kind. Study hard; play hard. Be in earnest. Be self-reliant. Read good books. Love your fellow man as your God; love your country and obey the laws; love truth; love virtue. Always do what your conscience tells you to be a duty, and leave the consequence with God.

TALLEYRAND.—Much has been written about the mental peculiarities of the Prince Talleyrand. The academician, M. S. Bueve, in a late study, gives the following curious details on the physiology of the Prince; "He had the singular faculty of sleeping but little; he passed the night at cards or in talking. He rarely went to bed before four o'clock in the morning, and yet he was up again at an

Aerial Locomotion.

We had the pleasure of being present, Friday morning, at the first trial of the "Avitor" or flying machine, which has been more or less before the public for sometime past. The test was made at Millbrae Station, where the Avitor works are located. We are unable, for lack of space, to give any detailed description of the machine. It is simply a model, of course an experimental one, 27 feet long and presents the general appearance of a corpulent sausage with pointed ends, clad in a waterproof jacket, and dragging the blades of an old-fashioned windmill behind it. This windmill addition is simply the steering apparatus by which the "avitor" is guided in either direction, or elevated or depressed. The propelling power is in two screw wheels, one on each side, worked by a small engine located immediately beneath the large gas receiver, which gives buoyancy to the machine. Longitudinal planes are also used, which serve the purpose of stationary wings. The principles involved in the construction of the "Avitor" we will not attempt to explain; they are the combination of all those heretofore accepted in æronautics, with some additions and many improvements. The model possessed a gas capacity of 1,360 feet, and a total weight of 80 pounds. The gas supply was insufficient to raise the "Avitor" from the ground, but, as soon as the little engine started the propeller, the machine lifted itself from the ground, and gracefully commenced its flight through the air. It was kept from going out of sight by two cords attached to it, in the hands of persons on the ground. Its motion was regular, and without any of the swaying

E. A. Pollard on the Rebel Congress.

From the advancesheets of E. A Pollard's "Secret History of the Southern Confederacy," we extract the following:

There were other scenes of indecorum in the Congress, of which we may spare details, in one of which a member was flogged with a cowhide in his seat for some indignity or aspersion in social life. Half an hour after this dramatic display took place messages were flying to all the newspapers in Richmond asking that their reporters should make no mention of it, putting the request on the ground that the publication would degrade the character of the Confederacy, and might be construed as "giving information to the enemy!" There is no intention of satire or extravagance in stating this explanation of "contraband" matter; it was actually given by sapient Congressmen, and accepted by complaisant journalists. The newspapers were generally taught an obligation to put all Confederate affairs in roseate color, or to dress them up in the stiffest garments of dignity. To relate anything prejudicial to the Confederacy, to mention even a derogatory social incident, was to incur in the minds of certain vain and paltry, but numerous persons in the South, the charge of publishing "contraband" matter, or of at least lacking in proofs of Southern patriotism. It was thus, to an extent, that the reader of this day can scarcely believe that public opinion in the Southern Confederacy was disarmed, and a wretched Congress passed almost unchallenged and unnoticed through a history of vile excesses and flagitious scenes.

TEA THAT COMES TO THE UNITED STATES.—We were in a tea house at

The Daily Oregon Statesman.

VOL. 13. SALEM, OREGON, THURSDAY, MARCH 12, 1874. NO. 34.

Daily Oregon Statesman.

S. A. CLARKE, Publisher.

Published Every Evening, Except Sunday.

PRICE By the Carrier, 25 cents per week.
By Mail one year, Eight dollars.
By Mail Six Months Five dollars.
By Mail Three Months, Three dollars
ADVERTISEMENTS On liberal terms.

TELEGRAPHIC.

EASTERN NEWS.

Death of Senator Charles Sumner.

WASHINGTON, March 11.—Yesterday in the Senate Senator Sumner had a slight attack affecting the nerves of his heart, but when he returned home was sufficiently well to entertain his friends at dinner, at the close of which he made allusion to the condition of his heart, and between 9 and 10 P. M. he was taken so sick as to require the attendance of physicians. An hour or more after he had a second attack of his old disease, *angina pectoris*. Several of his nearest personal friends were sent for and remained with him during the night. He passed a quiet night under a subcutaneous injection of morphine. This morning, at 9 o'clock, he was sleeping under it without material change. Surgeon General Barnes and Drs. Johnson and Lincoln were at that hour in consultation at the residence of the Senator. At 12:15 Mr. Sumner was fast failing. In addition to his physicians, Senator Schurz and Representatives Pierce and Geo. F. and E. R. Hoar were present, and Dr. Brown Sequard had been telegraphed for and was on his way to the city. At 2 P. M. Senator Sumner was still sleeping, though at intervals he would awaken, at which times he was in great pain. He was perfectly conscious when awake and knew all his friends, occasionally rallying to the effort of saying a few words to them.

3 P. M.—Senator Sumner has just died.

Oregon Steam Navigation Company vs. Winser et al.

WASHINGTON, March 10—In the United States Sureme Court.—Oregon Steam Navigation Company vs. Winser et al. In error from the Supreme Court of Washington Territory. Plaintiffs in error sued to recover $75,000, as stipulated, damages for an alleged breach of covenant, the averment being that in May, 1864, the California Steam Navigation Company, engaged in the transportation of freight and passengers on the waters of that at the point of death with the disease of pleuro-pneumonia. At last accounts, however, his condition had improved and hopes were entertained of his recovery.

SACRAMENTO, March 11.—A gang of ruffians infest this city who waylay and rob persons at night in quiet localities. On Monday night a man was knocked down and robbed of seventy-five cents, all he had, on Sixth street; he was also severely beaten. Last night, on Fourth street, a man was robbed of a silver watch and $40, and at the corner of Fourth and O streets another man was robbed of $50 and a gold watch.

LACONNER, March 11.—A Lightning Creek dispatch says the washes for the week are: Spruce Company, 101 ounces; Van Winkle, 118 ounces; Victoria, 100 ounces; Vancouver, 198 ounces; Point, 78 ounces. The Victoria Company are sinking another shaft, which is now down about 30 feet. The Vulcan company are down about 75 feet. The Costello Company expect to have their machinery at work in about eight days. Companies on outside creeks are getting to commence work.

VICTORIA, March 11.—The steamer Eliza Anderson sailed last evening and the Otter this morning, both for Cassiar, carrying away about 125 passengers.

The steamer California, from Stika, passed down this morning. She brings no news of any importance from Cassiar.

DIFFERENCE IN LOTS.

"It is a common thing," said the late Frederick Robertson, "to hear sentimental wonderings about the unfairness of the distribution of things here. The unprincipled get on in life; the saints are kept back; the riches and rewards of life fall to the lot of the undeserving. But if you look into it, the balance is perfectly adjusted even here. God has made His world much better than you and I could make it. Everything reaps its own harvest, every act has its own reward, and before you covet the enjoyment which another possesses, you must first calculate the cost at which it was procured. For instance, the religious tradesman complains that his honesty is a hindrance to his success; that the tide of custom pours into the doors of his less scrupulous neighbors in the same street, while he himself waits for hours idle. My brother! do you think that God is going to reward honor, integrity, high-

The Oregon Messenger

VOLUME 4. SALEM, OREGON, THURSDAY NOVEMBER 25, 1915.

GOOD POSITION TO BE FILLED

GOVERNOR WILL HAVE $3,600 APPOINTMENT AT HIS DISPOSAL NEXT MONTH.

MARSHALL MAY SUCCEED HIMSELF

Believed That Labor Member of Accident Commission Will Be Reappointed.—Status of Other Members.

A fat plum will be ready to pick at the state house about the first of the year and there is much gossip as to who the lucky winner of the highly desirable place is to be. The position to be filled is that of member of the Industrial Accident Commission now held by Wm. A. Marshall of Portland, whose term expires on the first Monday in January. However, the law provides that the appointment shall be made on the first Monday in December preceding the date of the expiration of the commissioner's term.

Mr. Marshall has held office since the organization of the Commission in November, 1913, and is now the chairman of the body. While there is considerable quiet rivalry for the place, which pays $3,600 per year, it is thought that Mr. Marshall will be reappointed, as he is the labor representatve on the board and is said to have almost the solid support of that element.

In addition to this fact in his favor, it is pointed out that Marshall is without question the strongest member of the Commission. Harvey Beckwith, one of the other members, a Democrat and holdover from the West administration, has never been conspicuous for his ability and it is predicted that

SALEM CHICKENS WIN PRIZES

Eugene Prescott's Salmon Faverolles Take Firsts and Seconds In Competition With the World

Eugene Prescott, of this city, has been apprised of the news that his choice Salmon Paverolles chickens have been awarded three first and two second prizes, out of five awards at the Panama-Pacific expasition in competition with birds England, France and Eastern states of this country. These are among the most important prizes to have been offered in the entire poultry exhibit. Mr. Prescott's awards were: First cockerel; first hen; first pullet; second hen and second pullet.

AGED STAYTON LADY DEAD.

Mrs. Margaret A. Weddle died Tuesday evening at her home at Stayton, aged 82. She had been paralyzed and nearly helpless for the past two years. She was the mother of eleven children, six of whom survive—one daughter in California and four sons and one daughter in the Willamette Valley. One son, O. L. Weddle, is at the Salem hospital, where he was recently operated on for appendicitis and where he will soon have another operation for some stomach ailment.

Funeral services for the late Mrs. Weddle will be held at Stayton Friday at 11 a. m., Rev. R. L. Putnam of the Christian church officiating.

BOYS' CONFERENCE TOMORROW.

The Older Boys' conference will convene in this city tomorrow afternoon and continue over Sunday. About 350 boys are expected to attend from all over the state and the committee in charge is desirous of securing accommodations for them in Salem homes during their stay here. An elaborate program has been prepared for the conference including addresses by some of the most prominent men in public and private life in Oregon.

NEW CHEESE FACTORY

What's the Matter with Salem?

Some people say its lack of a payroll.

Some think it is high taxes due to our spell ofextravagance a few years ago.

Others have still different reasons to offer for the depressed business conditions.

For there's no use denying the fact that business is—well, to put it mildly—rotten, and that the city is not thriving as it should.

No doubt many elements enter into the matter but we believe that the most serious handicap under which the city is laboring is its falure to take care of the products of the surrounding farms.

Sometime Salem may become a manufacturing city, but for many years to come it must derive its income in very large part from the surrounding farming country—which is not excelled anywhere on the coast for productivity when properly cropped and cared for.

In the face of these facts, we offer the farmer absolutely no inducement to bring his produce to this city to market. There appears to be a sentiment among some of the merchants of this city that the farmer is a necessary evil, to be tolerated but not to be given a square deal unless the farmer is on to the ropes and insists upon the full market price for his produce.

Take the meat question for instance: One farmer tells the Messenger that recently he wanted to sell several fine veal calves. He went to the Salem dealers and could not even get an offer. He shipped the calves to Portland, where they were snapped up at a good price and a request made for more. Another man killed several hogs without inquiring about the local market and when he tried to sell them in Salem he found it impossible. He went back home and put them in brine.

The same is true of fruit and practically everything the farmer raises. The local dealers—operating in combination in some cases, it is said—refuse to buy unless they can get the products of the farm at their own price, which is frequently so low that the farmer goes back home and lets his crops rot in the fields.

Until this condition is overcome, it is worse than useless for us to shout "Try Salem First," and to rail at the farmer for sending his money East for his necessities.

The problem must be met in a broad and liberal spirit of helpful co-operation. If it is not, we need not be surprised to see the "mail order" era followed by the "co-operative marketing" era, with its stores in this and other cities, financed and managed by the producers themselves.

It's up to us to look the problem squarely in the face and to find the remedy.

In the meantime the Messenger would be glad to hear from some of

INDEPENDENCE FERRY BROKE

Farmer Has Narrow Escape From Collapse of Huge Cable Support—Damage Is Being Repaired.

The falling of the big pole which supports one end of the wire cable for the Independence ferry, put the ferry temporarily out of business a few days ago during a high wind. A farmer who was waiting in his wagon to cross on the ferry was missed by the falling pole by only two feet, the horses having started just as the pole fell, otherwise he would have been probably crushed to death. The pole, which is about 80 feet high and very heavy, very nearly demolished the wagon.

NEWS IN A NUTSHELL.

WHITE CROSS VIBRATORS ($11.50 to $35.00) Call and see them and get free folder. Lockwood's, 216 North Commercial street.

* * *

County Roadmaster and Mrs. W. J. Culver have returned from an extended visit to the expositions at San Francisco and San Diego.

* * *

Hazel M. Stough has been granted a divorce from Ralph Stough upon the ground of cruelty. They have one son, aged 4, and no property interests.

* * *

Clarence Amos, of the U. S. S. Chattanuooga, is home in Silverton this week on a visit wth hs parents. He arrived Wednesday morning and is on a 20 days' furlough.

* * *

Supt. Smith and Luther J. Chapin gave an interesting agricultural meeting at Keizer School on Thursday evening to a full house. Slides were used to illustrate subjects.

* * *

Durbin & Cornoyer, agents for Wigan-Richardson & Co., hop factors of London, shipped a carload of Oregon hops to England on Tuesday. They are routed via Montreal.

* * *

R. A. Lucas has resigned as local agent of the prudential insurance company and accepted the position of district agent for the Columbia Life

NEW BRIDGE NEXT YEA

NEW BRIDGE FUNDS TO BE CLUDED IN 1916 BUDGET—INCREASE LIMIT.

APPROXIMATE COST, $233,(

Courts of Two Counties Agree Course of Action.—Property Values Decrease Over $1,000,000.

At a joint meeting of the Polk Marion county courts, held at court house yesterday afternoon, was decided that a new bridge acr the Willamette to supplant the old is a dire necessity and provision its construction will be made n budgets of the two counties for year 1916. It is not probable t actual work of construction will gin until May or June of next y following the normal Spring flo but it is proposed to complete structure before the close of the y The present structure, in course of pair, will last until a new bridge built.

If the steel-concrete type of bri is decided upon, which is in unanim favor of the courts, the approxim cost will be $233,000 of which amo Marion county will bear two-thir or about $155,000, and Polk cou one-third. In making provision the bridge the Marion county co will be privileged to increase the cou ty tax levy to an amount not exce ing 6 per cent above the levy for 19 the highest in the past two years.

The total amount raised in 1913 w $399,662.79 for all county purpos A six per cent increase of this amou would be $23,979.76, making the to

Gervais is a small farming community fourteen miles north of Salem, located on French Prairie which consisted of thousands of acres of rich, fertile land. John Wesley Thornbury, a Mexican War veteran, was an early pioneer in Gervais who came from Alabama. This photo shows his beautiful home, taken sometime before the coming of the railroad in the 1870s, and some of his family members *(left to right)*: Fred Baker, hired man; Albert Henniger Thornbury, son; John Wesley Thornbury, father; Sarah Esther Thornbury (Rothrock), wife; Lillian Elva and Virginia Olive Thornbury, daughters.

Gervais in Marion County was the home of Bruno Keppinger's Boot and Shoe Maker, a one-man business operated from his home in 1870. Keppinger learned his trade in Germany before coming to the United States. When he and his family moved to this country, they first settled in St. Louis, Missouri, then came to Gervais before the arrival of the railroad in 1870. His family members are *(left to right, bottom)*: Joseph Valentine Keppinger, son; Bruno Keppinger; Catherine (Ferschweiler) Keppinger, wife; and Nicholas Keppinger, son. On the balcony: Anne and Susie Keppinger, daughters; Peter, John and Michael Keppinger, sons; and Ira Hubbard, husband of Susie.

This confectionery store in 1909 also housed the home telephone office, all owned and operated by Joseph Valentine Keppinger, pictured here.

The history of Woodburn and the Willamette Valley is linked very closely with the development of transportation. Jesse H. Settlemier laid out the town shortly after the arrival of the Oregon & California Railroad in 1870. There are many theories as to how the town of Woodburn in Marion County got its name. Some say Mr. Settlemier saw a "wood-burning" locomotive and from that came up with the name. This photo from 1905 shows some of the residents of Woodburn waiting for the arrival of the daily train in front of the railroad station.

A photo of Main Street in the small community of Turner shows the Baker Hotel, owned and operated by Elijah and Sarah O. Baker, with the stage ready to leave for Stayton. The Holsey R. Miles livery stable is behind the hotel. Mill Pond *(foreground)* furnished water power to operate two flour mills and one sawmill.

THE TURNER TRIBUNE

VOLUME XXII   THURSDAY, JULY 15, 1937   No. 46

HAMMAN STAGE LINE NOW RUNNING TO BEND OVER SANTIAM HIGHWAY

Saturday morning the Hamman stage line started its initial trip from Salem to Bend over the new Santiam highway by way of Detroit and Breitenbush Hot Springs.

Daily service with one trip each way will be given. The Salem-Breitenbush bus will connect at Detroit with a second bus that will make the daily run from Detroit and return.

This new trip over the Santiam pass is one of the most scenic in the northwest, according to Floyd Hamman, who made a trip over the route last week. He found the route in surprisingly fine shape with only three miles of rough going.

The Bend-Detroit bus will be in the capable hands of Ed Hamman, brother of the late Joe Hamman pioneer stage man. Ed is a careful driver, having operated stages for the past fifteen years without an accident.

The Salem bus, operated by Floyd Hamman, will leave Salem daily at 10 a. m., meet the Bend bus at Detroit and continue on to

ATTENDS REUNION AT BRYANT PARK, SUNDAY

Mr. and Mrs. Cordell Ball and sons Keith and Robert, Mr. and Mrs. Emir Ball and children Edwin and Jean, Mrs. Frances Ball, Mr. and Mrs. Mayro McKinney and granddaughter Ruth Rawlings attended the fifteenth annual McKinney reunion held in Bryant Park, at Albany Sunday.

Mrs. Johnson, who makes her home with Mrs. Frances Ball, was also in the group.

Two of the surviving four children of William and Martha McKinney, pioneers, were present, Mrs. Frances Ball and Mayro McKinney. Mrs. Onie Longsworth, of Portland was unable to be present as was Mrs. Martha Adams, who left Portland recently for Baltimore, Md., to make her home with her daughter Mrs. Edna Riches and family.

Mrs. John McKinney and Mr. and Mrs. Archel Presnell of Salem, also attended. There were five visitors over 80 years of age present. Among them Mr. and Mrs. T. Shanks who came from Texas with their son: Frank Shaw of Seattle and Billy Cockran of Albany who celebrated

The Old Folks
At Home

There's a vast difference between "An Old Folks Home" and that line from the tuneful melody—Swanee River—which ends with "The Old Folks at Home!" The two are far apart, indeed. And yet an Old Folks Home all too often holds all the hope and happiness of countless sweet old ladies and gentle old men, who have found their way into charitable institutions in the winter of life.

Companionship and comfort is all that old age has ever asked, after the fires of youth are spent, and those poor souls who live their final years in a "charity" institution or poor-house—labeled an "Old Folks Home" are to be pittied, indeed. There may be homelike retreats here and there, with an understanding and sympathetic management, but it is common knowledge that most old men's homes, old ladies' homes and old people's homes are dreary places—the natural result of sour-faced political management which fits in with the somber surroundings and strict rules.

Very seldom do we find old people's homes. Pretty generally the sexes are divided. There is less companionship and more lonliness about one of these poor-houses—dignified by the name of "home"—than in any other spot on earth. Many an old father and mother, rather than be what they consider a burden to their children, seek refuge in these institutions while they wait for the "White Horse and His Rider." And in all too many instances they might as well be in jail. If you want to see disappointment, controlled bitterness, a sort of haunted and hungry look, a tired longing without hope, you will find it in the faces of old age in a charity institution. Sad, indeed, is the condition you will find in all too many so-called homes for the age.

The answer to it all is "Old Age Pensions." And the time will come when here in America there will be no more

JUNIOR BOYS CONFERENCE NEXT ON PROGRAM AT TABERNACLE

The Pioneer Assemblies of God Camp meeting opened here Tuesday with about 500 present for the first day's meeting and more arriving all the time. Elder W. P. Gaston is the guest speaker and each afternoon a children's church is being held.

Sunday will be Young People's rally day and a large crowd is expected. Sixty tents are on the grounds to accommodate many who have come to camp and all of the dozen or more nice cabins are being occupied. Three nice brick stoves were built by members of the Assembly and will be left to be used by those to come later.

Two large tents are being used for sleeping quarters and meals can be had at reasonable rates.

The Junir Boys Conference, sponsored by the "99 classes" of the Christian churches, will be held at the Tabernacle from July 25 to August 8, when one hundred boys are expected to enroll for the Conference.

August 16 to 22 the eighteenth

Three ladies check their trunks at the Salem railroad station in 1900, shortly before the departure of a Southern Pacific train enroute to California. Pictured are *(left to right)*: station baggageman; Mrs. Lillian McCully; Leah Orsella Guiss Patton; Mrs. Laura Ashby; and Harry David (Hal D.) Patton.

MORROW COUNTY

TWENTIETH YEAR   HEPPNER, OREGON, THURSDAY, JUNE 18, 1903.   NO. 943

DAYS OF SORROW IN HEPPNER

Awful Destruction of Life and Property Caused by Cloudburst.

141 BODIES HAVE BEEN RECOVERED

The Dead and Missing Number About 250 ---2000 Men Now Engaged in Relief Work Here.

Without a second's warning, a leaping, foaming wall of water, 40 feet in height, struck Heppner at about 5 o'clock Sunday afternoon, sweeping everything before it and leaving only death and destruction in its wake.

Nothing in the history of the Western country can compare with the awful disaster, and it can only be realized by eye witnesses.

In the middle of the afternoon dark clouds commenced to appear in the south and a short time before the flood a heavy rain fell

Ayers, Frank Roberts and several others. The family came down on a ladder and were taken out uninjured.

By this time the terrors of the flood could be realized. In the channel of the creek the wall of water was at least 40 feet deep and the crest of the stream seemed to be at least ten feet higher than the overflow on the sides. Dark and muddy, lashing like a storm at sea, houses were picked up like feathers. Up the buildings would go, spinning around like crashing to pieces like they were

onto the roof and they floated to shore.

Dan Stalter, who lost his wife and six children, escaped with one of his children by getting into a dry goods box that rode the waves and fortunately washed to the shore.

The water was at its height for only about an hour, and while the waters were receding, the survivors were organizing and search was immediately commenced for the missing.

The waiting room of the First National bank and Roberts' hall was transformed into receptacles for the dead and when the searchers were forced to quit by darkness, many bodies were recovered. At the first approach of daylight the entire town was out. Nobody slept. All were anxious to again commence the search that has been going on ever since.

Before the rushing torrent had reached the depot Leslie Matlock and Bruce Kelly two expert horsemen and old range riders appeared.

"May God, Lexington and Ione, can we beat the flood," were the words of Matlock waving a wire cutter in his hand.

Not a soul thought it could be done.

were out of hearing, clash went the

many thousands more.

Many ranches including buildings and crops have been ruined.

The loss to the business portion while not to be compared with the residence portion will foot up thousands of dollars.

A portion of the east side of Main street was flooded and the buildings were lifted from their foundations to the street almost blockading the thoroughfare from travel.

The town is now well organized for the dispatch of the immense amount of work.

Public meetings were held Tuesday and Wednesday evenings and different committees were appointed to take charge.

Mayor Frank Gilliam, Geo. Conser and E. M. Shutt comprise the executive committee with office at C. E. Woodson's law office, and they are doing grand work.

J. A. Woolery, of Ione, is a great worker, in fact, there are hundreds who should be mentioned.

The work of clearing out the debris, and the search for the missing is now progressing in a most satisfactory manner. The workers are apportioned in squads and a foreman for each squad and the work is systematic.

Mrs Ada Curtis.
Chinaman.
Chinaman.
Chinaman.
J H———
Carl Denis.
Chinaman.
Mrs Dawson.
Mrs Percy Dawson.
Percy Dawson's boy.
Percy Dawson.
J R Dawson.
Lloyd———
Bianche Estes
Mrs Wm Estes
Mabel Elliott
Florence French.
Nora Flareon.
— Farmer
Bertha Fristoe
A. McGahu.
A C Giger.
Mrs Lillie Hamilton.
Harry Hamby.
J L Hockett.
Hazel Haynes.
Mrs Banson Hart.
Mrs Hamby.
R F Hynd's little girl.
Bert Hynd.
Mrs Robert Hynd.
Mabel Howard.
Mary Howard.
Mrs M B Haines
J J Harr's
N Howard
Mrs Thos Howard.

On June 14, 1903, a sleepy hot Sunday evening in the town of Heppner, a cloudburst descended as a flood on this small farming community. In a period of twenty minutes following the collapse of a local dam, the water poured through the town resulting in a loss of 225 lives.

This photo, taken a day or so after the terrible Heppner flood in 1903, shows the Union Pacific railroad station surrounded by rubble. The agent for the railroad and his wife both drowned trying to escape. Had they remained in the two-story station, their lives would have been spared, as this structure withstood the flooding waters.

MULTNOMAH COUNTY

On the Way to the Portland Automobile Club's First Show.

The automobile comes of age! The first automobile show ever held in the Pacific Northwest was held in March, 1909. This had been one of the aims of the Portland Automobile Club since it was organized early in 1905. Some of the early cars were weird-looking contraptions which sputtered along with firecracker-like noises frightening many people as well as horses, dogs, and chickens. Prone to mechanical trouble, they often broke down causing spectators to laugh and to jeer, "Get a horse!"

A cartoon in an Oregon newspaper states that the war in Europe might cause the price of gasoline to go up to $.40 a gallon. We hope it never reached that outlandish price!

A 1908 Stoddard-Dayton touring car in front of a home in Portland. Note the carriage house for a horse and buggy in the background and the statue on the curb for tethering a horse.

MICHIGAN
Breaks Record

Makes Portland-to-Tillamook Run in 4 Hours and 47 Minutes

¶ THIS DEMONSTRATES the speed, durability and reliability of the MICHIGAN. Although a speed of from 40 to 48 miles per hour was maintained over the corduroy roads and 55 to 59 miles over other parts, the machine is none the worse for its trip and is now on exhibition at our salesrooms.

FULLY EQUIPPED, F. O. B. PORTLAND, $1350

Michigan Auto and Buggy Co.

The Michigan was a large car manufactured in Detroit for only four or five years beginning in 1909.

The Best Way To See Portland

Is by Tally-Ho, Cabriolet, Boulevard Wagon or Landau

Sizes to Accommodate 4, 6, 9, 16 and 28 People

The Oregon Auto Stage Terminal, opened in 1922, was located on the northeast corner of Park and Yamhill Streets. It was the first centralized bus depot in Portland. The buses here are fourteen-passenger buses belonging to the Portland-Salem Stage Line and the Columbia River Stage Line. John L.S. Snead, manager of the terminal, helps with loading the 1918 Overland *(center)*. This converted vehicle has a chassis built for a truck as evidenced by the front wheel with nine lug bolts holding the tire. The bus to the right is a 1920 White. To the rear is the first Unitarian Church, while in the extreme background is a portion of the Oregon Journal building, now called the Jackson Towers. The brick wall to the right is that of the Heilig Theatre.

An advertisement appearing in the *Portland Telegram* in 1897 read: "Studebaker Brothers Manufacturing Company, East Third and Morrison Streets in Portland. The above interior depicts the finest carriage repository in the West. The Portland house carries phaetons, landaus, broughams, cabriolets, rockaways, farm and ranch wagons, road carts, heavy-spring wagons. They also carry imported harness, robes, whips, and stable utensils."

Fifth and Yamhill Streets in 1904 showing the Portland Cable Railway Company open-air car built in the 1890s *(left)*. It has since been converted to use electric power. The Depot-Jefferson car *(right)* was built in 1903 for the Portland Railway Company. The U.S. District Court building *(rear)* is now the Pioneer Post Office and the oldest public building in the Pacific Northwest.

In 1912 *The Portland Evening Journal*, later called *The Oregon Journal*, moved into its own twelve-story building located on the southeast corner of Broadway and Yamhill Streets.

The U.S. Frigate *Constitution* nearing Portland in 1933. The history behind this old ship is quite interesting:

1797:   The U.S. Frigate Constitution was commissioned
1803-05:   Engaged in war with Tripoli
1812:   Captured H.M.S. Guerriere and H.M.S. Java
1815:   Captured H.M.S. Cyane and H.M.S. Levant
1828:   Condemned and ordered broken up or sold
1830-31:   Oliver Wendell Holmes' poem "Old Ironside" had aroused such public indignation and the people demanded she be saved.

Old Ironside

Ay, tear her tattered ensign down!
Long has it waved on high,
And many an eye has danced to see
That banner in the sky;
Beneath it rung the battle shout,
And burst the cannon's roar;
The meteor of the ocean air
Shall sweep the clouds no more.

Her dock, once red with heroes' blood,
Where knelt the vanquished foe,
When winds were hurrying o'er the flood,
And waves were white below,
No more shall feel the victor's tread
Or know the conquered knee;
The harpies of the shore shall pluck
The eagle of the sea!

Oh! better that her shattered hulk
Should sink beneath the wave;
Her thunders shook the mighty deep,
And there should be her grave;
Nail to the mast her holy flag,
Set every threadbare sail,
And give her to the god of storms,
The lightning and the gale!

Oliver Wendell Holmes   1830

The *U.S.S. Portland* in 1934 passes under the beautiful St. Johns Bridge in Portland. The district of St. Johns is in the background. Built in 1933, this heavy cruiser is 582 feet long and according to Naval records "it was said to be a bad roller." The suspension bridge was dedicated on June 13, 1931, and was built at a cost of $4,250,000. It is 3,833 feet long and 205 feet above the Willamette River at the center of the main span.

U. S. S. PORTLAND

THE OREGONIAN.

Equal Rights, Equal Laws, and Equal Justice to all Men.

T. J. DRYER, EDITOR. PORTLAND, O. T. WEDNESDAY, DECEMBER 4, 1850. VOL. I NO. 1.

The Oregonian printed its first edition in a shack at Front and Morrison Streets in Portland in 1850, nine years before Oregon became a state.

The stone marker above the grave of Thomas Jefferson Dryer, founder of *The Oregonian*. This gravesite is located in Lonefir Cemetery in Portland.

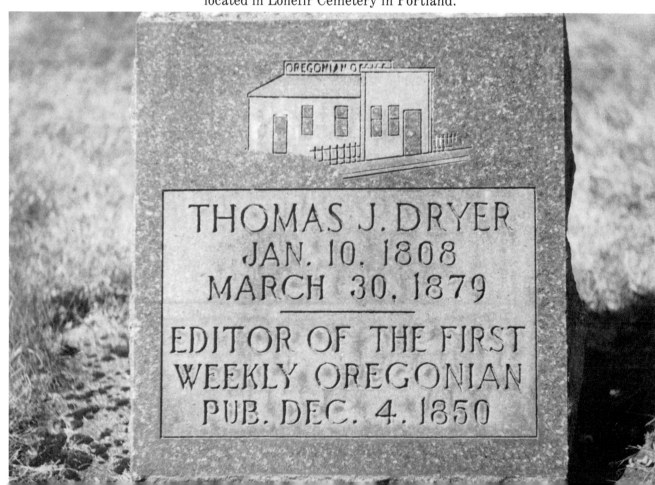

THOMAS J. DRYER
JAN. 10, 1808
MARCH 30, 1879

EDITOR OF THE FIRST
WEEKLY OREGONIAN
PUB. DEC. 4, 1850

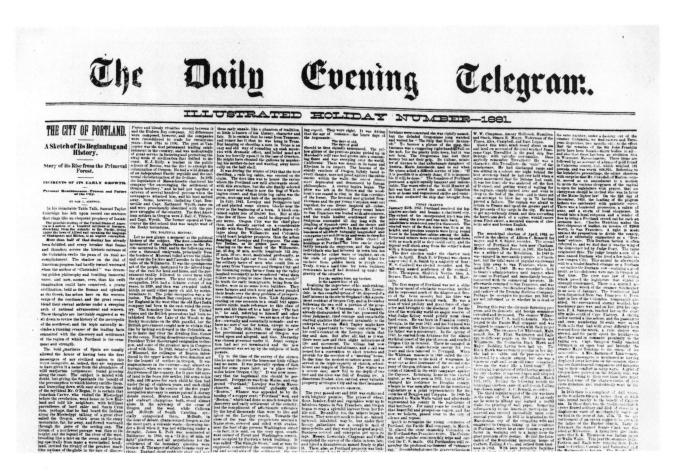

National as well as international news was covered in Volume One of Portland's evening newspaper.

EXTRA THE EVENING TELEGRAM. EXTRA

VOL. XLIV.   PORTLAND, OREGON, SUNDAY FEBRUARY 5, 1899.   NO. 97.

GRIM WAR BREAKS OUT
IN THE PHILIPPINE ISLANDS

Aguinaldo's Followers Attack the American Forces at Manila and are Repulsed.

Filipinos Were the Aggressors and Made a General Attack on American Outposts.

FIGHTING STILL IN PROGRESS

The Engagement Opened at 8:45 Saturday Evening----The Cruiser Charleston and the Gunboat Concord Bombarded the Enemys Lines----Americans Make a Gallant Charge and Capture Several of the Positions of the Enemy

THE INDEPENDENT REPUBLICAN.

OPPOSED TO PARTY BOSSISM.

VOL. 1.   PORTLAND, OREGON, WEDNESDAY, MAY 16, 1894.   No. 2

Platform and Principles of the independent Organization.

WHEREAS, The foundation upon which the Republic of the United States was built is the right of the Elective franchise and the perpetuity of its government in all its various branches depends upon the just and proper exercise of that right. It confers a privilege upon the recipient of the grant of right, but, like every other privilege bestowed for the public good it also imposes a duty, the moral obligations of which are of a very high and important nature, requiring that elections of public officials be honestly conducted and the voter be allowed to exercise his choice conscientiously and intelligently.

WHEREAS, This city and county for a long time have been dominated by bossism and ring rule in the conduct of political affairs, the aim of which has been to ignore the duty incident to the privilege of the elective franchise, and to prevert into a machine system to secure spoils and boodle, and which, if allowed to flourish will render elections a farce and sap the foundations of the Republic itself. Therefore be it

RESOLVED, That we favor the preservation of the Australian Ballot law as it now stands and the enactment of a strict registry law.

2nd. That we are opposed to the various departments in our city government, notably the police, fire, and street cleaning department being manipulated in political affairs.

3rd. We demand an economical administration of the finances of this city

Northup, Myers and Paxton,

Their Records in The Legislature.

Enemies of Honest Elections—Violators of the Constitution—Paxton and Myers Charter Manipulators.

H. H. Northrup has rushed into print. Mr. Northrup wishes to defend his record. This calls attention to the fact that Mr. Northrup has a political record. During the last legislature, when the infamous Portland city charter was passed, Northrup, with Paxton and Myers—all candidates for re-election on the straight Republican ticket—were representatives from Multnomah county.

Voters, examine the records of these men!

Take Paxton, for instance. The man concerning whom the legends tacked on the poles of the General Electric Co. read "Vote for O. F. Paxton for state representative." Paxton was chairman of the delegation from Multnomah and

The two last named are lawyers, they should understand the constitution.

House bill 382, among other things, appropriates: "For the aid of St. Mary's Home near Beaverton, $2000; for the aid of the Sister of Good Shepard of Magdalen Home, Portland, $4000." Giving, donating, dispensing the taxpayers' money to private religious institutions! Did Paxton vote for it? Did Myers vote for it? Did Northup—this Northup who prates about his record—did he vote for it? See page 979 journal of the house. On bill No. 382, among those voting aye, were Paxton, Northrup, Myers! Voters, it is a matter of record! They cannot deny it. Unconstitutional, illegal, the appropriation of public money to private religious institutions, and these men voted for it. Voters, do you want Paxton, Myers and their ilk boosted into a position where they can misappropriate public money again? Think over these things. We are looking up records. House bill No. 175 was the Durham election bill. It was the embodiment of the old "chalk mark," a dollar-a-head ring plan. It was to do away with and wipe out the present Australian ballot law. The ring wanted the "dollar mark" style. House bill No.

THEN AND NOW.

From the *Morning Oregonian*:

SUNDAY, APRIL 19, 1891.

"With a fire department run by one political boss, (Lotan) and a police system run by another, (Simon) each depending upon the influence which he can wield through his holdings to sustain himself and defeat the other, it is no wonder that these departments are each more expensive and disereditably managed than the other. Of the fire department, however, it may be said that it is, if needlessly and reprehensibly costly, reasonably efficient when called into action and that when the gong sounds it is there, while the police system is as notoriously inefficient as corrupt and expensive."

SUNDAY, APRIL 8, 1894.

"It was the recognized fitness of Joseph Simon for legislative work, and the acknowledged fact that in the present state of our affairs we must have such legislation in the direction of economy and retrenchment as the times demand, that caused so many citizens to ask him to become a candidate for the senate once more. Not only the affairs of our city and county, but the affairs of the state, require the presence of men in the legislature who can do things, and whatever Mr. Simon undertakes he attends to.

Judging from the oft repeated remark: "It's awful tough to swallow Joe Simon," as made by some of our best Republicans, the "many citizens" who asked him to become a senatorial candidate becomes a ridiculous assertion. Were it not for the fact the people are surfeited with Democracy and the consequent, al-

Oregon Weekly Times.

BY CARTER & AUSTIN.   PORTLAND, OREGON, MAY 8, 1858.   VOL. VIII—NO. 26

Oregon Weekly Times.

ISSUED EVERY SATURDAY MORNING

BY WM. D. CARTER & R. D. AUSTIN.

Business Cards.

DR. R. B. WILSON,

DOCTOR A. G. HENRY.

DR. W. WEATHERFORD.

The Kansas Question—Report of Hon. A. H. Stevens, of Ga., from the Select Committee of Fifteen.

(Concluded from last week.)

Indian Difficulties.

PACIFIC CHRISTIAN ADVOCATE.

THOMAS H. PEARNE, Editor.   WM. ROBERTS, A. F. WALLER, G. HINES, C. S. KINGSLEY, J. H. WILBUR, PUBLISHING COMMITTEE.

VOL. III, NO. 35.   PORTLAND, OREGON—SATURDAY, MAY 8, 1858.   WHOLE NO. 139.

Thomas Paine.

A Good Story—if True.

A Needless Waste.

A Good Man Gone.

Never Forgotten.

Jesus a Counsellor.

A Beautiful Incident.

Evil Speaking.

Jonathan among the Spirits.

"Oh! Such Fine Singing!"

Charles Lamb's Warning.

PORTLAND DAILY TIMES.

VOL. 1. NO. 2. PORTLAND, OREGON, MONDAY, OCTOBER 31, 1898. 3 CENTS. PRICE ON ALL TRAINS FIVE CENTS

WHISKY'S WORK

Moonshiners and Informers at War.

TROOPS ORDERED OUT

A Battle Royal is Confidently Expected Soon.

PROPERTY IS BEING BURNED

The Situation One of General Alarm and Consternation in Cleburn County and a Great Loss of Life and Property is Feared in the District Before Troops Arrive.

Little Rock, Ark., Oct. 31.—Cleburn county is on the verge of a local war that threatens to assume gigantic proportions. For several years this county has been suspected as being the locality in which moonshine whisky in large quantities was being manufactured. The revenue officers have been tireless and indefatigable in their efforts to stamp out the illicit traffic and to this end have enlisted a number of informers to assist them. The moonshiners have discovered this fact, also the names of many of the informers and are thirsting for revenge.

In order to accomplish this over 100 of these dealers in illicit whisky have

PROTOCOL SIGNED.

Boundary Dispute Between Chili and Argentina Settled.

New York, Oct. 31.—A Buenos Ayres dispatch says that the protocol providing for a settlement of the boundary dispute, which at one time brought Chili and Argentina to the verge of war, has been signed.

THE REINA MERCEDES.

Wreckers Are Now At Work Trying to Float Her.

Santiago, Oct. 31.—Wreckers today began the work of raising the Reina Mercedes, which was sunk by Spaniards in the mouth of the harbor. Work on the Colon continues.

THE MARIA TERESA

En Route to the United States Under Her Own Steam.

Washington, Oct. 31.—The Infanta Maria Teresa, the Spanish warship recently raised at Santiago by Hobson, has started for Norfolk, Va., under her own steam. She will arrive by the end of next week.

A SQUARE BACKDOWN.

The Fashoda Incident to be Settled in England's Favor.

Paris, Oct. 31.—The Eclaire announces that the Fashoda question will be settled immediately and in a manner favorable to England.

OREGON AND IOWA.

These Two Crack Ships Nearing Their Destination.

Washington, Oct. 31.—The Oregon and Iowa are expected to arrive at Bahia, Brazil, tomorrow.

RIOT IN JERUSALEM

Whey Pawnbrokers Fall out "The Devil's to Pay"

'TIS ALL IN THE FAMILY

ONE CENT A MILE

Lopped off Passenger Rates

IN EFFECT TOMORROW

Big Saving to be Made in Northwestern Travel

PORTLAND IS BENEFITTED

Reductions to Affect Local Rates in Washington and Idaho on the Northern Pacific and O. R. & N. Co's. Lines and Between Points There and Stations in Oregon.

Tomorrow morning a new schedule in passenger rates will go into effect on the lines of the Oregon Railway and Navigation Company's lines in Washington and Idaho. There will be a general reduction in local fares from 5 to 4 cents a mile.

The new rate sheets have just been received from the printer. While fares from and to points in Oregon are not effected, tickets from any point in Oregon to any point in Washington and Oregon, and vice versa, can be purchased at the cut rate. All local travel within Washington and Idaho will come under the reduction.

Under the revised schedule fares between Portland and Spokane are re-

STEAMBOATS "QUEERED."

A Long Series of Accidents on the River Recently.

A veritable hoodoo appears to have taken possession of the river during the past few months. The number of boats disabled has been unusual and is causing old river front men to shake their head and prophesy further disasters.

First the Regulator was blown upon the rocks near the entrance to the Cascade locks and badly damaged. Scarcely had the wreck of the steamboat been removed than the Hattie Bell experienced a similar fate on almost the same point of rocks.

The third boat to meet misfortune was the Hogue near the locks at Oregon City, and following this accident came the terrilbe disaster on board the torpedo-boat Davis, which cost the lives of seven men. The tugboat Sampson, although not wrecked had an accident to her boilers by which the engineer, James W. Hare, was tepmorarily disfigured.

The latest addition to the list was the collision between the steamers T. J. Potter and Geo. W. Shaver, which resulted in the latter being sunk.

All told, there were several hundred people on board the various boats at the time the casualties occurred, but with the exception of the Davis tragedy no lives were lost.

Such a number of mishaps taking place so close together, in point of time, has never before happened in the annals of local steamboat circles and the old timers have come to the conclusion that some sort of spook is getting in its fine work. It is a strange coincidence that in no case has anyone been found to blame.

PHILIPPINES OR BUST

Uncle Sam Insists on the Entire Group.

GIVE THEM UP OR FIGHT

GET OR FIGHT

The Ultimatum is Laid Down to Spain

NO MORE FOOLISHNESS

Given Until Next Friday to Say Yes or No.

MUST BE DECISIVE ANSWER

That Part of the Debt Contracted on Behalf of the Philipine Islands Will be Assumed by the United States But Will Not Assume One Dollar on Other Proposition.

Paris, Oct. 31.—The joint peace commission after a session lasting one hour today adjourned until next Friday, in order to give the Spaniards time to prepare a reply to the United States' note on the Philippine question. The note presented by this government announces the fixed purpose of America to take the entire Philippine Islands and to assume that part of the debt which was contracted for on behalf of the islands. The United States positively refuses to assume any part of the debt which was contracted for in the effort by the Spaniards to suppress the insurrection. This is the ultimaatum of the United States and in consequence there will be no more negotiations of a different charac-

When the democratic committee met Saturday night a report from the treasurer was read stating that there was no money on hand with which to conduct the campaign of Mr. Flanders.

Both the democrats and the populists have candidates running upon practically the same platform, the abolition of the present charter or radical changes in its form. The only reason the pops give for not supporting Flanders is that he is a gold man, and then in the same breath they say that the money question does not elnter into the matter.

NEW CITY CHARTER.

Printed copies of the new charter have been received from the printer and are now to be had at Auditor Gambel's office. A number of lawyers and politicians called at the city hall to secure a copy today and are diligently comparing it with the old charter to ascertain changes. So far no complaints have been registered against the new law by those who have examined it thoroughly. One of the changes receiving attention is the reduction of salaries and the section which is creating all the talk regarding the city finances with relation to the payment of warrants. The famous section is as follows:

"Provided, that no warrant shall be drawn, signed by the mayor, or attested by the auditor, until the money for payment thereof is in the hands of the city treasurer, appropriated to the payment thereof upon presentation of same."

THE WHITE CROSS SOCIETY.

The President of the Society Has Arrived at Omaha.

The president of the White Cross society has arrived at Omaha, and will be back within a few days. A report on the working of the society will then be published.

FRANCE'S MINISTRY,

Dupuy Succeeds in the Forming of a Cabinet.

RIBOT REFUSED PORTFOLIO

DEATH ON RAIL

Terrible Train Wreck in Canada.

KILLED AND MAIMED

The Victims are British Soldiers and Sailors.

PROPFRTY LOSS VERY LARGE

The Special Train Was From Halifax and Bound for Vancouver with Officers for the North Pacific Fleet at Esquimalt When it Jumped the Track

Montreal, Oct. 31.—News has just been received here of the disastrous wreck of a special train which left Halifax Thursday last for Vancouver with marines and officers for ships of the British North Pacific fleet at Esquimalt. The train ran off the track near Margaret station and is a complete wreck. So far as heard from two sailors named Miller and Frickney are killed, and Samuel Harrison and Thomas Burns seriously injured. Samuel Smith was also fatally hurt. The property damage is very heavy.

HANDBOOKS FOR POLICE.

Officers to be Furnished with a Synopsis of Ordinances.

The Portland Daily News

SIXTH YEAR. PORTLAND, OREGON, TUESDAY MORNING AUGUST 7, 1888. 20 CENTS PER WEEK

THE DEAD SOLDIER.

The First Arrangements Made for Sheridan's Funeral.

MESSAGES OF CONDOLENCE

Pouring in for the Silent Patriot's Widow.

THE GENERAL'S BOOK.

The Last Pages Soon to Go to Press. General Schofield to Assume Command.

By Pacific Postal Telegraph.

NONQUITT, Mass., Aug. 6.—Everything is quiet around the Sheridan cottage to-day. At 2 o'clock this morning the embalmers who had been summoned from New Bedford arrived and took possession of the body.

As illustrative of the confidence felt by Mrs. Sheridan in the ultimate recovery of her husband, only a few days ago she sent to Chicago money to pay off a small mortgage on real estate owned by the General in that city, and that she had made some preliminary arrangement with a view to the permanent removal of the General from Nonquitt early in September, fearing the cold winds of Autumn might retard his speedy restoration to health.

THE FUNERAL AND BURIAL.

This evening it was arranged that ...

EASTERN NEWS ITEMS.

Amalgamation Favored.

MINNEAPOLIS, Aug. 6.—The second general meeting of the railway employes to consider the proposition for the confederation of the Locomotive Engineers', Firemen's and Brakemen's Brotherhoods and Switchmen's Mutual Aid Association, convened here yesterday. The gathering included representatives from eighteen divisions of engineers, thirteen lodges of firemen and eight lodges of brakemen. Four lodges of switchmen represented between 7000 and 10,000 men. The meeting was almost unanimous in favor of amalgamation. Steps are being taken to further the result.

Killed by Lightning.

PRESTON, Minn., Aug. 6—During an extremely severe electrical storm here yesterday, Magnus Johnson and two children were instantly killed by lightning. When the storm became violent the family started to take refuge in the cellar. Johnson and two children were just at the top of the steps when the lightning struck the house, tearing through the roof and hurling all three to the cellar.

The "Bard" Broken Down.

MONMOUTH PARK, Aug. 6.—The Bard, who until Thursday last was recognized as the champion of the turf, has broken down as a result of the race that day in which he was beaten by the California horse Firenzi. His off hind leg failed shortly after the race and he was unable to stand until the afternoon. The ligaments of the leg are badly strained and it is feared he will never be able to race again.

California Fruit Auction.

Yellow Fever Spreading.

Train Wreckers at Work.

CONGRESSIONAL.

Several of the Pacific Coast Bills Reported Favorably.

UNIVERSAL SORROW

Expressed on Receipt of the News of Sheridan's Death.

THE HOUSE AND SENATE

Adopt Resolutions Expressing Their Regret of the Death of the Hero of the Shenandoah.

By Pacific Postal Telegraph.

WASHINGTON, Aug. 6.—In the Senate to-day Palmer reported, with no amendments, the bill appropriating $60,000 for a fog signal apparatus outside of the bar of the Columbia river, Oregon; also the bill appropriating $12,000 for a lighthouse and fog signal at Tatoosh island, W. T., and the bills appropriating for lighthouses at Heceta head, Siuslaw river, Oregon, and Gray Harbor, W. T., $80,000 and $60,000 respectively.

The bill for the relief of the State of Oregon for equipments, etc., for Union soldiers in the War of the Rebellion, has been reported on adversely by Stewart, as was also a similar bill for the relief of Colorado, Oregon, Nebraska, California, Nevada, Idaho and Washington.

Resolutions of sympathy similar to ...

CABLE NEWS ITEMS.

The Porte Notified.

CONSTANTINOPLE, Aug. 6.—The Turkish Ambassador at Berlin has notified the Porte of negotiations between Germany, Austria and Italy on the Bulgarian question soon to be begun. Also that the coming meeting between Degiers, Russian Minister of Foreign Affairs, and Bismarck, will lead to the holding of a congress at Berlin, the deliberations of which will be confined exclusively to the Hungarian difficulty.

Still Raining.

BERLIN, Aug. 6.—The rain continues in torrents. Reports from the provinces say that the floods are beginning to subside. Terrible damage has been done to the crops. Many head of cattle were lost at Konigsberg, Elbing and Sagan. Railways are interrupted at Gorlitz and Bromberg. Great damage has been done to property in many places.

The Strike Continues.

PARIS, Aug. 6.—The strike of Parisian laborers continues, and over 10,000 hands are now idle. ... the presence of armed troops at various points in the city, who have orders to use their arms at the sligtest disturbance, has had a kind of quieting effect.

Refuses to Wear Clothing.

LONDON, Aug. 6.—Ex-Empress Charlotta of Mexico is becoming more furiously insane, and refuses to wear clothing. Her attendants are obliged to use force to overcome her opposition.

Dillon Denied a Writ.

ALONG THE COAST.

John McNulty, Convicted of Murder in San Francisco.

HE TURNS INSANE

And Tries to Murder the City Physician.

TWO BODIES RECOVERED.

The Remains of Jo and Ben Thelmer Found Near Eugene, Oregon—A Fruit Peddler Killed.

By Pacific Postal Telegraph.

SAN FRANCISCO, Aug. 6.—John McNulty, the 'longshoreman who shot and killed James Collins, another longshoreman, during a trivial quarrel, a short time ago, was convicted of murder in the first degree this morning, the jury being out one hour. The verdict leaves no alternative but the passage of the sentence of death upon him.

About 3 o'clock this afternoon the convicted murderer became temporarily and violently insane. He was discovered foaming at the mouth. When the cell door in the county jail was opened he tried to kill the city physician and others who were restraining him. Three-quarters of an hour elapsed before his struggles ceased sufficiently to put a straight jacket on him.

VICTORIA NOTES.

CALIFORNIA NEWS.

DIAMONDS At Wholesale.

The attention of the RETAIL JEWELERS Of the Northwest is asked to my importation of personally selected

Fine Diamonds Direct from Amsterdam.

The general public are cordially invited to examine the jewels, which include many rare gems.

A. FELDENHEIMER, Cor. First and Morrison Sts

Clearance Sale —OF— SUMMER SUITS.

We will sell the remainder of our Summer Suits at Prices never before offered here. We buy at lower rates than any other house in the Northwest, and, quality considered, can and will undersell them all. In proof of this, see our corner window and the prices at which we offer suits:

$27 00 Suit reduced to $20.
25 00 Suit reduced to 18.
22 50 Suit reduced to 16.
20 00 Suit reduced to 14.
18 00 Suit reduced to 12.
15 00 Suit reduced to 10.

G. SHINDLER & CO., Furniture Manufacturers. Folding Beds, Parlor Sets, Bed Room Suits.

[Factory at Willsburg.]

G. SHINDLER & CO., Salesroom—166 First Street, through block, 200 feet, to 167 and 169 Front Street PORTLAND, OREGON.

A CHANCE FOR THE POOR! BIG CUT IN PRICES. OBSERVE OUR LIST OF FIGURES:

L. ZIMMERMAN, Butcher and Packer, 82 First Street.

THE U. S. BREWING CO. MANUFACTURES THE BEST Lager Beer and Porter IN THE NORTHWEST.

BATTLE OF GETTYSBURG. THIS GREAT CYCLORAMA IS NOW ON EXHIBITION Entrance on Third street, between Pine and Ash.

The Portland News

OREGON'S INDEPENDENT NEWSPAPER

2 CENTS on Streets in Portland

The Weather: Portland and vicinity: Fair tonight and Wednesday; little change in temperature; changeable winds. Temperature last 24 hours, 70-53.

If It Will Help Oregon—The News Is For It

Home Edition

TWENTY-FIFTH YEAR—NO. 191 Entered as Second-Class Matter at the Postoffice at Portland Oregon PORTLAND, OREGON, TUESDAY, MAY 5, 1931 On Trains, Boats and News Stands, Five Cents Phone: ATwater 4151

NEWS AND TELEGRAM TO MERGE

An Announcement by The Portland News

THE PORTLAND NEWS today announces the purchase of all the capital stock of the Portland Telegram, Inc. As soon as final arrangements are completed, which will be in a very few days, the Telegram will be merged with and become a living part of The News, and the merged newspaper will be known as The News-Telegram.

In carrying on the negotiations which resulted in the merger, The News has had but one thought: that it will now be possible to give the people of Oregon a better, more complete and more vital liberal newspaper than would have been possible under two managements. At the same time a complete afternoon circulation coverage is made possible to advertisers.

The developments of the past few years have shown conclusively that three afternoon newspapers overcrowded the Portland field, that newspaper energies were being dissipated too widely to give the best possible service to the people. The situation hampered the development of such a liberal newspaper as Portland, and Oregon, deserve.

Merging of The Portland News and the Portland Telegram does not mean the death of either newspaper, rather it means that the best elements of both will be combined in a more perfect newspaper. The best features of both will be retained in The News-Telegram, including the United Press and the Associated Press news services, and many other departments. The operating staff of The News-Telegram will be greatly increased and many of the present members of the Telegram organization will join the merged newspaper.

In the handling of the news, The News-Telegram will strive to be fair, and unprejudiced at all times. It will give every man a fair hearing whether it agrees with him or not.

The News-Telegram will be published from the present office of The Portland News at Fifth and Main sts.

PROBE OF BOND HOUSE HERE COMPLETED

Mott Submits Findings to Van Winkle for Opinion; $400,000 Involved

SALEM, Ore., May 5.—(Special Correspondent.)—An investigation of the activities of the Municipal Reserve and Bond co., Portland, forced into receivership last December during a suit instituted by stockholders, has been conducted by the corporation commission and now awaits the opinion of Attorney General Van Winkle.

Corporation Commissioner Mott admitted Van Winkle was considering the case Tuesday. Mott refused to release any of his findings, or any of the complaints made against the company.

The company handled municipal and improvement bond issues and also sold installment bonds. Through its various activities it is understood to have accepted more than $400,000 of investors' payments.

H. A. Jansen, Portland, was named receiver of the company Dec. 27. Jansen is understood to have been in Salem several times and is known to have consulted with Mott over the situation. It is also reported he consulted Governor Meier. No confirmation could be received for these reports.

Persons familiar with the case are of the opinion the corporation commission, and Jansen are attempting to make the company's executives make full settlement.

PROPOSED TAXI LAW OPPOSED

Cab Operator Declares Many Drivers Will Be Thrown

Breakdown Suffered by Clara Bow

Vivacious Screen Star Taken to Sanitarium; Doctors Order Rest

HOLLYWOOD, Cal., May 5.—(U.P.)—Clara Bow, film star, was placed in a sanitarium after a nervous collapse on a set at her studio and her condition is regarded as serious, it was announced by Paramount-Publix and her physician today.

Miss Bow was rehearsing her current picture with other members of the cast last Sunday night when she suffered a breakdown, it was said. When it became apparent that she was in a serious nervous state she was taken to the Glendale sanitarium.

Two physicians, Dr. Wesley Hommel and Dr. Victor Parkins, consultant, were in attendance.

Rest Imperative

They joined today in the following statement:

"A complete rest is imperative. Miss Bow is suffering from shattered nerves. It would be dangerous for her to make a picture at this time. The trouble can only be overcome by a complete rest."

B. P. Schulberg in charge of West Coast production for the studio, announced that work on Miss Bow's picture, an adaptation of David Belasco's "The Woman" was suspended indefinitely.

During the last year Miss Bow has featured in a number of situations which severly taxed her nerves.

For several months she was in the limelight in an alleged $30,000 settlement to the wife of a young Texas physician, Dr. Early Pearson, who she met in Hollywood.

Nerves Under Strain

This incident was followed by the Cal-Neva gambling adventure in which the star assertedly lost $13,000 and stopped payment on the checks on the ground that she had been told $100 chips she played with were only worth 50 cents each.

Another ordeal for the star came when she was called to testify at the grand theft trial of Daisy De Voe, once her friend and secretary. Miss DeVoe was convicted of steal-

BOARD VOTES TO PURCHASE SCHOOL SITE

$2,500,000 West Side High Gets Authorization After Stormy Session

Climaxing a whirlwind campaign of organized west side parents for a $2,500,000 high school, the school board Tuesday began negotiations for the necessary property.

The new school will be located either on the Kamm tract at 14th and Madison sts., or on the Multnomah Amateur Athletic club property and stadium.

The school board Monday night decided to buy one or the other by a 4 to 3 vote.

Refusing to be thwarted by attempts of opposing members of the board to delay commitment by causing further investigation, the parents with a salvo of oratory secured the necessary legislation.

Cigar clenched between champed teeth, Director J. Fred Staver led the opposition to the resolution offered by Director William F. Woodward.

Leaping to his feet, Staver told ex-Governor Oswald West, representing the parents, "You can't threaten us."

West immediately advanced to the directors' bench, shook his fist under Staver's nose and replied, "My child is going to have decent treatment in this school system—you can take that as a threat or any damn way you please.

"You're going to give us what we

(Continued on page 2, column 3.)

TRAIN RUNS OVER TEACHER, TOTS

Woman Saves One Child, Gives Life Trying to Rescue Other Two

No Stage Life for Her, Says Marguerite Sperry

"The only way to be happy," opines Marguerite Sperry, 15-year-old Spokane, Wash., miss, "is to work hard at the things you like to do." And she does just that, putting in hours daily singing, dancing, playing the piano, violin and saxophone, and going to high school. She has filled various engagements in Spokane vaudeville houses, but has

DEAL IS CLOSED LATE MONDAY EVENING

News Buys Portland's Oldest Evening Daily; Best Features of Both Retained

THE PORTLAND NEWS today announced the purchase of all of the capital stock of The Portland Telegram, Inc. While the Telegram will continue to be published for a few days at its present building, as soon as arrangements can be made it will be merged with The News and the merged newspaper known as The News-Telegram.

Plans for the merging of the two newspapers were not completed until late Monday night, following conferences between representatives of The News and the Telegram.

Herbert F. Fleischhacker, president of the Anglo and London Paris National bank, of San Francisco, principal stockholder of the Portland Telegram, returned to California Monday night following signing of the papers.

Fielding Lemmon, editor of The News now, will be editor of The News-Telegram, while Harry W. Ely, business manager of The News, will act in the same capacity for The News-Telegram.

Advantages Cited

Representing the Scripps-Canfield newspapers and The Portland News were:

E. W. Scripps, treasurer; Harry W. Ely, president of The News Publishing co.; R. J. Benjamin, editor-in-chief of Scripps-Canfield papers in the Pacific northwest; Fielding Lemmon, editor, and Daniel E. Powers, attorney for The News.

John Veach of Joseph, Haney & Veach, represented Fleischhacker and C. H. Brockhagen, editor and publisher of the Telegram.

An outstanding advantage to sub-

The News-Telegram

The Portland News Combined With PORTLAND TELEGRAM

2 CENTS on Streets in Portland

The Weather: Portland and vicinity: Unsettled tonight or Thursday, slightly cooler tonight, north and northwest winds: 86, 54.

Oregon's Independent Newspaper

Home Edition

TWENTY-FIFTH YEAR—NO. 192 Entered as Second-Class Matter at the Postoffice at Portland Oregon PORTLAND, OREGON, WEDNESDAY, MAY 6, 1931 On Trains, Boats and News Stands, Five Cents Phone: ATwater 4151

Today

Mexico's Great Day
King George's 21st Year
Now The Day Is Over
Mr. Mellon Speaks

By Arthur Brisbane

(Copyright, 1931, by King Features Syndicate)

Yesterday, May 5, Cinco de Mayo, good Mexicans celebrated the victory that freed their country forever from European control.

Patriotic Mexicans (no nation is more patriotic) lifted their glasses in gratitude to the memory of the French defeat, establishing the fact that Mexico is for Mexicans.

Mexico's May 5th should make real Americans thoughtful, now that so many Americans seem eager to discard George Washington's teachings and join the European League of Nations or world court for instructions as to the management of the United States.

Mexicans will never make that mistake.

* * *

While the Mexicans were celebrating their important holiday, King George of England was celebrating the end of his twenty-first year as king. Only 17 English kings and queens have remained longer than 21 years on the throne. King George has now equalled the term of William the Conqueror. His has been a different term. The conqueror ruled. He suppressed many small kingdoms to make a big one, wiped out villages and farms to create vast deer parks.

Long after his death, late as the time of Henry the Second, an English workman moving from one parish to another in search of a job, without permission, was branded on his flesh with a red hot iron.

King George has lived to see a workman, formerly in the coal mines, prime minister of England, and writing the speeches that the king delivers, "the address from the throne."

We may see changes as great here, we may even see the citizens themselves running the country, something we haven't seen yet.

* * *

George F. Baker, one of the most powerful workers in American business and finance, was buried yesterday. "Abide With Me" was sung and "Now the Day Is Over."

Men of power in the world that interested Mr. Baker were there. Senator Dwight W. Morrow, just back from Sicily; Charles E. Mitchell, chairman of the National City bank; Charles M. Schwab, Chief Justice Charles Evans Hughes. There were also railroad presidents and their conversation about business after the funeral was none too cheerful.

Some that were too optimistic at the beginning of our slump are now taking it too solemnly, as though

CLYDE ATTACK FIZZLES OUT IN COUNCIL

Attempt to Put Commissioner "on Spot" About Market Brings Talk

An attempt to put Commissioner Ralph C. Clyde "on the spot" because he opposed an emergency ordinance for the erection of the public market fizzled out in city council meeting Wednesday morning.

The session in Mayor Baker's office last week, when organized labor and proponents of the Front st. site tried to rush through the proceedings, was thoroughly hashed over, with the mayor, Clyde and Gust Anderson, secretary of the Central Labor council, all explaining their stands.

Charges Inconsistency

Even the firm of Carey & Harlan was brought into the verbal barrage when Dan Malarkey, representing the Front st. interests, charged that Clyde was inconsistent in his attitude toward emergency ordinances because he had voted for the emergency ordinance employing them.

"Certainly I voted for that emergency ordinance," shouted Clyde. "The people expressed their desire for municipal ownership when they elected me. The people were in favor of speeding up public ownership when they voted for me and the employment of Carey & Harlan was a step in that direction."

Clyde precipitated matters in the midst of the council's proceedings when he announced there was a threat to "put him on the spot" and that he was willing for it to start at any time. Clarence Hynerson, editor of the Labor Press, got the floor and admitted he was probably the one meant by Clyde, but said he had nothing to say at the present time.

Not "Star" Chamber

Mayor Baker emphasized that the meeting in his office was not a star chamber session; that he often held such informal conferences with

(Continued on page 2, column 3.)

TWO CARS SEEN AT ACCIDENT

Witness of Death of Harry McGuire Upsets Theory Held by Police

"I saw two cars there—one McGuire's overturned car." With these

An Open Letter

To the People of Oregon:

The new News-Telegram greets you.

In it are merged the fine traditions and liberal principles of two newspapers that have served Portland, and Oregon, for generations.

Bear with us, please, for the mistakes that will be made during the first few days, while the blending of the two newspapers and organizations is in process.

For Portland, the merger means progress, better, surer, more capable journalism in the common cause.

For the devoted men and women who have produced The Portland News as an honest, valiant newspaper, it means the realization of dreams and worthy ambitions, the opportunity to serve you with larger ability.

For those equally devoted men and women who have been inspired by the worthy traditions of the old Telegram, rooted in a half-century of Portland's growth, this tensely trying week means something else. The death of a newspaper is a heart-breaking experience to those who have worked and sweated for it, and loved it.

Yesterday, with chaos around them, they "carried on" in the finest tradition of newspaperdom. Personal doubts and uncertainties, the unknown tomorrow—all were brushed aside in courageous fulfillment of the duty of the hour—to go through to the finish with a flag flying high. They produced, out of all the turmoil, that final issue of the Telegram, a good newspaper to the last inch of type.

Great roaring presses and intricate machines and massive buildings are not newspapers. The newspaper is its heart, its soul, its fighting spirit, and if it has none, then it is a dead and nameless thing no matter how luxuriously it may be equipped and housed.

The presses and the machinery and building of the Telegram are relatively unimportant. It is the grand old liberal spirit of the newspaper itself that counts, that is what The News-Telegram proposes to perpetuate as a living part of itself.

Many of the able men and women of the Telegram, who carry its spirit in their hearts, will find welcome, and larger opportunity, in the merged News-Telegram organization. Every effort will be made to utilize fully all the ability and energy and loyalty of the two staffs, devoting their joint product, the new Portland News-Telegram, to the great days of a greater Portland.

Many Battles Fought In Newspaper's Life

FIRST EDITION OF NEW PAPER OUT TODAY

Combined News-Telegram With Best Features of Both Goes to Press at 8 A. M.

The Portland News, published for 25 years under that name, and The Portland Telegram, oldest afternoon paper in Portland, published 55 years as The Telegram, appeared today combined as The News-Telegram.

Following completion of the largest newspaper merger ever consummated in Portland, The News took over the capital stock of The Telegram late Monday. The state edition Wednesday was to be the first of the merged papers.

First street and mail editions of The News-Telegram were to appear about 9 a. m., followed by the home edition, the complete paper, at 2 p. m.

Several days additional time will be required before the new system is thoroughly worked out. The News-Telegram, now holding the Associated Press afternoon franchise and the United Press afternoon service, offers to its readers a state, national, and world service entirely complete.

Advertisers Benefit

Advertisers will be benefitted by the combine, which will place a larger, more active, liberal newspaper in the afternoon field.

Editorial directors of The News-Telegram, now affiliated with the Scripps-Canfield league of newspapers, will devote several days to selection of leading features of the two papers. Among the choice features saved will be the Brisbane editorials. Other syndicate releases, cartoons, departmental material, and direct correspondence services are to be decided upon soon.

E. W. Scripps, treasurer of the Scripps-Canfield league, and R. J. Benjamin, northwest editorial direc-

(Continued on page 2, column 5.)

OREGON LEADERS LAUD MERGER

Officials and Business Men See Great Opportunity for New Liberal Newspaper

Civic, commercial and financial leaders, as well as high officials in public life, today lauded the con-

Rose Queen's School Picks Its Candidate

Rachel Atkinson

Alma Mater of 1930 Floral Monarch Comes Forward with Candidate

UP where big statues and little statues of Abraham Lincoln greet the visitor on every turn, the student body hopes to repeat its last season's victor in naming the Rose Festival candidate who will score in the annual election.

And so it follows Rachel Atkinson, 17, with a bit of Nordic strain, has been named. Her selection does not change the order of things. She is blonde, blue-eyed and of Nordic descent. So are the other

SHORTS COVER

FUGITIVE MAY BE LURKING IN OREGON

Escaped Woman Convict Is Reported Seen in Eastern Part of State

BOISE, Idaho, May 6.—(U.P.)—Prison authorities today were investigating a report from an eastern Oregon rancher that Lyda Southard, escaped murderess, was seen walking on the highway yesterday morning near Ontario, Ore.

The rancher said the woman answering Mrs. Southard's description was hitch hiking. She was picked up by a motorist and taken to Huntington, where she obtained another ride from a man driving a large car. The second car was last seen proceeding over the Old Oregon trail toward La Grande.

Residents of the neighborhood said they noticed lights flashing near the prison Monday night, apparently signals to the woman within.

The escape came as a complete surprise. Mrs. Southard was a model prisoner and since her imprisonment has not been involved in any trouble.

Mrs. Southard was convicted of murdering her fourth husband, Edward Meyer, in Twin Falls, Ida., 13 years ago. She was suspected of murdering her first three husbands and also the brother-in-law of her first husband. At her trial the state introduced evidence purporting to show she poisoned the four men and collected insurance after the death of each.

The jury convicted her of second degree murder after 24 hours deliberation. Eleven jurors, it was learned, favored first degree. One held out and the second degree conviction was a compromise.

Mrs. Southard maintained her innocence throughout. She claimed the death of Meyer was through drinking contaminated water. The

(Continued on page 2, column 5.)

CHILD IS SLAIN BY MANIAC

Woman Drags 5-Year-Old Into Basement, Murders Her With Ax

AKRON, O., May 6.—(U.P.)—Louise Burleson, 5, was lured into the basement of a house today by a maniacal woman who chopped her

THE ONLY AFTERNOON NEWSPAPER IN PORTLAND THAT CARRIES ASSOCIATED PRESS DISPATCHES

THE WEATHER
Tonight and Tuesday fair; colder tonight with killing frosts.

THE EVENING TELEGRAM

TELEGRAM PHONES
Broadway 200   A6781

42D YEAR.   CITY EDITION.   PORTLAND, OREGON, MONDAY, NOVEMBER 11, 1918.   PRICE ON TRAINS, NEWS STANDS AND IN OUTSIDE CITIES, 2 CENTS. ON STREETS, 2 CENTS.   NO. 180.

GERMAN SURRENDER COMPLETE, STRIPPED OF MILITARY POWER

WAR END BRINGS WILD REJOICING

Allied Armies Will Occupy Rhine Land

Portland Celebrates Peace With Delirious Joy

Good News Is Signal for Big Happy Event

EXCLUSIVE EVENING MEMBER ASSOCIATED PRESS

Average Net Paid Circulation of The Telegram for Six Months Ending March 31, 1931 . . . .

60,360

PRICE 2c TRAINS, BOATS AND NEWS STANDS OUTSIDE OF PORTLAND 3 CENTS

PORTLAND TELEGRAM
NEWSPAPER — PUBLIC SERVICE

FINAL HOME FINANCIAL
If your Telegram does not arrive by 6:30 p. m., phone BR 8484 and the paper will be sent.

55th Year   PORTLAND, OREGON, TUESDAY, MAY 5, 1931   No. 17

2 ARRESTED IN ALLEGED SWINDLE GAME

Today
Who Will Disarm First?
San Francisco's Week
Too Many Lawyers
Others Need Aid
— By Arthur Brisbane —
Copyright, 1931.

"DISARMAMENT is vital to the revival of business," said President Hoover to the international chamber of commerce, adding: "Of all proposals for the economic rehabilitation of the world, I knew of none which compares, in necessity, or importance, with the successful results of general disarmament.

General disarmament, if feasible and if those agreeing to it would act loyally, would save many billions a year.

But who will disarm first? Why not let those begin disarmament who have started all the important international wars of a hundred years past. This country has never started one.

When it was suggested that the death penalty be abolished, a witty Frenchman replied: "Que messieurs les assassins commencent." "Let the assassins commence."

In disarmament, the war makers might commence.

SAN FRANCISCO celebrate "Achievement Week," and, wisely, it concentrates on efficient advertising what San Francisco and all of California have done, and wonderful results produced.

ACHIEVEMENT today consists in doing something worthwhile, and letting the world know by advertising that you have done it. Have had the people want, then tell them you have it.

California revolutionized the production and distribution of fruits and vegetables, creating a gigantic demand and supp. d, ti.

In the way of achievement San Francisco can point to its steady growth, financial power and great energy in skyscrapers and the ris-

NEWS BUYS TELEGRAM; TO LEAD FIELD IN PORTLAND

Announcing the purchase of the capital stock of The Portland Telegram, Inc., The Portland News today says:

The Portland News today announced the purchase of all of the capital stock of The Portland Telegram, Inc. While the Telegram will continue to be published for a few days at its present building, as soon as arrangements can be made it will be merged with The News and the merged newspaper known as The News-Telegram.

Plans for the merging of the two newspapers were not completed until late Monday night following conferences between the owners of The News and The Telegram.

Herbert F. Fleishhacker, president of the Anglo and London Paris National bank, of San Francisco, principal stockholder of the Portland Telegram, returned to California Monday night following signing of the papers.

ADVANTAGES CITED
Representing the Scripps-Canfield newspapers and The Portland News were:

E. W. Scripps, treasurer; Harry W. Ely, president of The News Publishing Co.; F. J. Benjamin, editor-in-chief of Scripps-Canfield papers in the Pacific Northwest; Fielding Lemmon, editor, and Daniel F. Powers, attorney for The News.

John Veach of Joseph, Haney & Veach represented Fleishhacker and Brockhagen.

An outstanding advantage to subscribers of the two newspapers will be the combining of leading feature services in the one publication.

Exclusive use of the Associated Press afternoon service, in conjunction with full United Press release, will assure complete coverage of ai news stories, local national and international.

Among other features to be in-

As One

Portland News and Portland Telegram to Be Issued As One Large Paper.

THE PORTLAND NEWS today announces the purchase of all the capital stock of the Portland Telegram, Inc. As soon as final arrangements are completed, which will be in a very few days, the Telegram will be merged with and become a living part of The News and the merged newspapers will be known as The News-Telegram.

In carrying on the negotiations which resulted in the merger, The News has had but one thought; that it will now be possible to give the people of Oregon a better, more complete and more vital liberal newspaper than would have been possible under two managements. At the same time a complete afternoon circulation coverage is made possible to advertisers.

The developments of the past few years have shown conclusively that three afternoon newspapers overcrowded the Portland field, that newspaper energies were being dissipated too widely to give the best possible service to the people. The situation hampered the development of such a liberal newspaper as Portland and Oregon deserve.

Merging of The Portland News and the Portland Telegram does not mean the death of either newspaper, rather, it means that the best elements of people's newspaper.

PLAN TO TAKE TARIFF OUT OF POLITICS GETS HEARING

WASHINGTON, D. C., May 5.—(AP)—Julius Barnes, who last week urged revisions in the Hawley-Smoot tariff rates, told the International Chamber of Commerce today it would be "most unfortunate" to reopen the tariff question in the next session of Congress.

Amplifying his discussion of the

(Concluded on Page 2, Column 2.)

members of The Telegram organization will join the merged newspaper.

Fielding Lemmon, editor of The Portland News, will be editor of the News-Telegram. Harry Ely, business manager of the News, will be business manager of the News-Telegram.

In the handling of the news, The News-Telegram will strive to be fair, and unprejudiced at all times. It will give every man a fair hearing whether it agrees with him or not.

Editorially, The News-Telegram will continue the well-recognized liberal policies which have actuated both The News and Telegram for so many years. It pledges itself to serve the best interests of the people; it hopes it will deserve to retain the confidence which the people of Oregon have placed in The News and The Telegram.

The publishers of The News-Telegram will try to produce a newspaper that will be as welcome in the homes of the loyal readers of The Telegram as in the homes of the many friends of The News. Actually, the publishers will be simply trustees acting for the people of Portland, for The News-Telegram will be the

Joins the Royal Family

Margaret Vogland, elected by her classmates at Jefferson high school as candidate for queen of Portland's Rose Festival. From eight girls, chosen at the various high schools, the ruler will be selected and the others will serve as royal princesses during the fete.—Telegram staff photo.

OREGON CITY MILL WORKER HELPS POLICE CAPTURE PAIR

OREGON CITY, Ore., May 5.—(Special.)—Charged with having worked an unusual confidence game to swindle John Novak, paper mill worker, out of $500, Fred Tomich and Fred Tanuse, Austrians, were in jail here today.

The sum of $500 was recovered by police.

According to Novak's story, Tomich arrived here a week ago, and after gaining his friendship, explained that he had been chosen to aid in an important mission concerning the aged father of Tomich, living in Texas.

A fortune teller had told the old man that he could regain his health only by distributing $5000 among the poor and needy. Tomich, said Tomich, explained the details of distributing $5000 to Oregon, and said he must first produce a similar amount to show good faith.

Novak told police he went to the bank yesterday and drew $500 from his savings account. This money, he said, he gave to Tomich, but en route to the expense office, where Tanuse promised a similar amount would be waiting, he became apprehensive and attempted to elude him.

He yelled for help and called on Police Warren, arrived on the scene in time to arrest Tomich. Tanuse was apprehended later as he attempted to board a train at Canemah.

Fate of 3 Youths On Murder Count In Hands of Jury

SPOKANE, Wash., May 5.—A superior court jury will be asked today to decide whether three youths must die on the gallows

FAMED BRITISH FLIER KILLED

Princess Ileana, Archduke Engaged
BUCHAREST, Roumania, May 5.—(AP)—Princess Ileana, 22-year-old daughter of Queen Mother Marie

RIFLE CLEW IN BRUTAL KILLING

IRVINGTON.

A BEAUTIFUL SUBURB TO THE CITY OF PORTLAND, OREGON.

CONNECTED BY ELECTRIC CARS.

TEN MINUTES RIDE.

Located on High Level Ground.

Pure Water for Household Purposes.

Ample Supply for Fire Department.

Will be on the Market May 1, '90.

C. H. PRESCOTT, *Trustee,*
A. L. MAXWELL, *Agent,*
THEO. WYGANT, *Secretary.*

Office, Hotel Portland. **PORTLAND, OREGON.**

Developers of the Portland suburb of Irvington issued this poster in 1888–1889.

This poster was printed in 1885, but the town of Sellwood did not become a part of Portland until 1893.

TOWN OF
SELLWOOD

Situated on the East Bank of the Willamette River, and Contiguous to the City of

PORTLAND, OREGON.

 LOTS

FOR SALE ON INSTALLMENTS OF

$10 PER MONTH

Officers Sellwood Real Estate Company,

PORTLAND, OREGON.

H. L. PITTOCK,................................PRESIDENT AND DIRECTOR
C. P. CHURCH,.........................VICE-PRESIDENT AND DIRECTOR
T. A. WOOD,...................................MANAGER AND DIRECTOR
F. O. McCOWN,..............................TREASURER AND DIRECTOR
N. O. WALDEN,...DIRECTOR
F. C. GOODIN,...SECRETARY

FULTON PARK!

PROPERTY OF THE SOUTHWEST PORTLAND REAL ESTATE COMPANY,

The Largest, Best Located and Most Desirable Tract Ever Placed upon the Portland Market.

SALE COMMENCED JUNE 20TH, 1888.

FULTON PARK is located one mile south of the present corporate boundary, and in the rapidly growing direction of the city.

FULTON PARK consists of fifteen hundred choice residence lots, 50 x 100 feet each, with full width streets and improved boulevards.

FULTON PARK is convenient to public schools and churches, and enjoys telephone and telegraph communication with the city of Portland.

FULTON PARK affords a charming view of Mount Hood, Mount St. Helens, Mount Jefferson and the rugged Cascade range.

FULTON PARK enjoys a perfect system of natural drainage, and is absolutely free from the baneful effects of malaria.

FULTON PARK is reached by the Narrow Gauge railway. Trains passing every fifteen minutes. Fare, five cents.

FULTON PARK is also reached by the Oregon & California railway, only ten minutes' ride from the Portland post office.

FULTON PARK is supplied with an abundance of the purest of spring water, as clear as crystal and as cold as ice.

FULTON PARK is located on Riverside avenue (White House road), conceded by everybody to be the most beautiful drive on the Pacific coast.

FULTON PARK affords a splendid view of the cities of Portland and East Portland and the beautiful Willamette river.

FULTON PARK is the future great residence site of the city of Portland, and affords a splendid field for investment.

FULTON PARK property, by reason of its convenient location to the city, will quadruple in value within two years.

FULTON PARK will be fully and correctly illustrated in the August number of THE WEST SHORE. Don't fail to secure a copy.

PRICE, TERMS, ETC.

Prices of lots in FULTON PARK range from $50 to $500 each, according to location. No deviation will be made from the printed price list, except on cash purchases, when a discount of five per cent. will be allowed. TERMS—One-fourth cash, balance in quarterly payments of twenty-five per cent. each, with interest on deferred payments at eight per cent. per annum. An advance of five per cent. will be made on the printed price list on the first day of each month for a period of twelve months, commencing September 1, 1888, thus insuring first purchasers an absolute profit of sixty per cent. per annum. Parties at a distance purchasing by mail or otherwise, in order to determine the amount of first payment, must add five per cent. to printed list after September 1, otherwise remittances will be returned at expense of sender. The title to FULTON PARK property is guaranteed to be absolutely perfect. All bonds and deeds will be furnished without additional charge.

For lithographic maps, printed price lists or other information, call on or address

PACIFIC LAND AND INVESTMENT CO., Agents,

No. 46 Washington St., Portland, Or.   J. T. FLYNN, Manager.

This advertisement for Fulton Park appeared in 1887.

This ad for Woodlawn appeared in *West Shore* in 1890.

WOODLAWN

Is located on the Portland & Vancouver motor line, on the high and sightly ridge

Midway Between Portland and Vancouver.

The fare is FIVE CENTS, including ferry, and the time occupied is TWENTY MINUTES. It is the finest suburban site for homes about

WOODLAWN

Was placed on the market

OCT. 14th, 1888.

Since that date **235** lots (all full size) have been sold, **22** neat and attractive houses built, a system of water works constructed to furnish every lot in the tract, and

Hundreds of Homes

Will be built this summer.

Lots MUST soon be worth $500 each and more.

PORTLAND

City Property

Our lists embrace the finest

BUSINESS

—AND—

RESIDENCE

Properties about the city, and all are invited to call and examine.

As Attested by Sales Already Made.

The prices of lots range from $250 to $400, all full size and every one perfect.

TERMS: $10.00 down; $10 00 monthly; no interest. Liberal discount for cash.

Remittances may be made by postal order or express, addressed to

BORTHWICK, BATTY & CO.,

No. 2 Washington St., PORTLAND, OR.

☞ Capitalists and others seeking investments should write for a copy of our special contract, in which we guarantee 10 to 15 per cent. net, according to terms and amount of investment.

"Where rolls the Oregon"

The Lewis & Clark
Centennial Exposition
and Oriental Fair

To be held at PORTLAND, OREGON
JUNE 1 TO OCTOBER 15, 1905

THE expedition of Captains Lewis and Clark, sent by President Jefferson to explore the great river of the West and its tributary region, laid firmly the foundation for securing the "Oregon Country" to the United States. The one hundredth anniversary of the arrival of the expedition in Oregon will be fittingly celebrated at Portland in 1905, by a great Exposition, designed to show the marvelous progress of the Pacific Northwest during the century, and to indicate the possibilities of the future. Oriental nations are to be fully represented, and one of the sure results of the Exposition will be the rapid increase of commerce with Asiatic countries.

When opened to the Public, the Exposition will represent a total outlay of $5,000,000.

1905

President	H. W. GOODE
First Vice President	I. N. FLEISCHNER
Second Vice President	A. L. MILLS
Third Vice President	SAMUEL CONNELL
Secretary	HENRY E. REED
Treasurer	FIRST NATIONAL BANK
Auditor	WM. R. MACKENZIE

Massachusetts State Building as it looked at the Lewis & Clark Centennial Exposition & Oriental Fair held in Portland, June to October, 1905.

At the close of the Lewis & Clark Fair, the Massachusetts State Building was moved in sections to a gently sloping site on Mount Tabor and reassembled. It was first used as a sanitarium and later purchased by Benage S. Josselyn, president of the Portland Railway Light & Power Company, who spent considerable money refurbishing it. He arranged for one of the Mount Tabor streetcars to stop on Belmont Street and be a part of the picture showing the beautiful home and the flowers surrounding it. Mr. Josselyn was transferred back East and the home and grounds were sold in 1913 for $85,000 to Anker Poulson Heningson, a native of Denmark who had become a national figure in the produce business. The house was razed in 1942.

All eyes at the Lewis & Clark Centennial were on the skies when eighteen-year-old Lincoln Beachey made the first controlled flight over Portland. It was the first powered, lighter-than-air craft to cruise Oregon skies. The lift was provided by a gas bag shaped like a watermelon. Beachey rode a spindly walkway beneath the belly of the balloon. A twenty-five horsepower engine pulled the contraption through the air. In order to climb, Beachey would go to the rear of the walkway and to descend, he walked forward. Note the word "Gelatine" on the side of the aircraft. It was built for the Knox Gelatine Company and was used to advertise their product.

Vista House is one of the many sights to be enjoyed while motoring on the world-famous Columbia River Highway. It is located on the crest of Crown Point sitting on a basaltic cliff 735 feet above the Columbia River in Multnomah County. This structure was dedicated in May, 1918, and built at a cost of one hundred thousand dollars. The end of the Oregon Trail for the early pioneers coming West was at The Dalles. To continue beyond this point was a real challenge for those early pioneers. Many constructed homemade log rafts and would move their families and wagons and other belongings down the river. The Vista House was built as a memorial to the early immigrants who had crossed the continent suffering from Indians, heat, and other discomforts only to lose their lives on these crudely-built rafts in the rapids of the mighty Columbia River.

Looking east on unpaved Powell Boulevard at the intersection of Main Street in Gresham, Multnomah County's second largest city as it looked in 1912. On the left side of the street *(left to right)*: First State Bank; Gresham Drug Store founded by Dowsett family with Dr. Wallace C. Belt, physician, sharing the building; L.L. Kidder's Hardware store; *Beaver State Herald* printed here at an earlier date. Right side of the street *(left to right)*: J.C. Hessel, agricultural implement dealer; Paul O. Hetzat, baker; on the corner, a saloon. A 1911 Overland touring car can be seen in the center of the street.

POLK COUNTY

Chartered, 1865.   Organized, 1866.

CHRISTIAN COLLEGE,

MONMOUTH,

Polk County, - Oregon.

A liberal Charter, granted by the State Legislature, confers all necessary powers on the Board of Trustees to preserve the rights and manage the affairs of the Institution.

The Location is Central, Accessible, Healthful and Beautiful.

It is reached by the O. R. W. (Limited), which passes through this place; and by the O. & C. R. R., which passes Independence, two miles east.

The Members of the Faculty are Competent, Energetic and Devoted to the Cause of Education

Annual Meeting of Board of Trustees, Tuesday before the 3d Sunday in June.

Tuition per Half Term---Ten Weeks:

Collegiate Department...$9 00
Preparatory Department....................................... 7 50
Janitor's Fee... 1 00
Music, (Piano)... ⎫ At Teacher's
    "   (Organ) .... ⎬ Prices.
    "   (Vocal)... ⎭

Payments, Invariably in Advance.

No Fees will be Refunded to Students Leaving Before the Expiration of the Term for which they have Paid, Except in Cases of Protracted Sickness.

Boarding can be obtained in Private Families at $3.00 Per Week.

For further particulars, address—
T. F. CAMPBELL, A. M., President.

— 1881 —

Monmouth in Polk County is a college town and its history is the story of the school. The town was settled by a group of Christian Church followers back in the 1850s. The college was given to the State of Oregon in 1891. From the beginning, the college was co-educational with most of the students coming from local tradesmen and farmers. Here is a list of the various names the college has used:

Monmouth University 1856
Christian College 1865
Oregon State Normal School 1882
Oregon Normal School 1911
Oregon College of Education 1939
Western Oregon State College ... 1981

Southern Pacific Train #34 stopped at Monmouth in 1905 to load U.S. Mail, Express and passengers for Portland.

Schedule: LV Airlie .... 7:30 AM
LV Monmouth .... 8:10 AM
AR Portland .... 3:05 PM

The track has been removed and this is now Jackson Street. The rear building *(right)* facing Main Street is Monmouth Improvement Building serving several stores and doctors.

Some of the 1890 class of the Oregon State Normal School at Monmouth posed in front of P.H.D. Murphy's Boarding House, located at Monmouth Avenue and Main Streets. Students shown are believed to be *(front row)*: Mary Blount, Carrie Hayden, and Callie Brodie; *(back row)* B.C. Altman, Charles Cochran, C.W. Barr, E.C. Keyt, and C.T. McArthur.

The Horace Lindsay and W.L. Hodgins Grocery and Confectionery Store on Main Street in Monmouth was built in 1870. Located upstairs was the Maples Hotel, run by David M. Hampton. Small building in the center is an insurance office, while to the right is P.H.D. Murphy's Boot and Shoe Shop. On the extreme right is Murphy's Boarding House. Taylor Halleck, a local carpenter, is in front without a coat.

The Monmouth Herald

Vol. I   Monmouth, Polk County, Oregon, Friday, September 4, 1908.   No. 1

SOME SCRAPS OF HISTORY

Monmouth, Past, Present and Prospective.

A GOOD PLACE TO GET YOU A HOME

A Great Fruit Country If Properly Developed—A Big Walnut Orchard.

The town of Monmouth was founded in 1855 by T. H. Lucas, S. S. Whitman, Elijah Davidson and I. F. M. Butler, the latter being still alive and a resident of the city. "Uncle Ira" has been identified with the town from its earliest inception to the present time, in fact he may be said to be the father of the town from the fact that he cast the deciding vote at a meeting of the Trustees when the town was named; naming it for Monmouth Illinois, his former home. The first house was built in 1855 by the trustees of Monmouth University, the fore-runner of the Oregon State

week for the fall run.

Our transportation is taken care of by the I. & M. Railway and we have four trains daily each way, giving us very good transportation facilities; in fact much better than many larger towns have.

Our close proximity to Salem, the State Capital, makes this a desirable location for those who have business to transact there and it is only a question of time when we will have electric rail connection with that city.

Land is cheaper here than in any part of the Willamette valley and the only reason it is so, is that this part of the state has not been exploited as have the others. We have as good soil as they and in many instances, better. Our fruits are as good when properly cared for, as any in the state and we have fine walnuts growing here; several large orchards having been set out during the past few years. J. B. Stump has a 75 acre walnut orchard and Ira C. Powell 11 acres, others have smaller ones and it is only a question of time when this place can well be said to be the "Walnut

MAKE CHANGES IN FACULTY.

Prof. Campbell Enters The Field Of Law

THE OREGON STATE NORMAL WILL HAVE

Capable Educators In President Riggs, of Drain and Mr. Fargo, of Pendleton.

The many friends of the Oregon State Normal no doubt have noticed press accounts of the changes in the faculty for the coming year. A. F. Campbell for the past 15 years a faithful teacher has left the profession and now has a law office in Eugene. Mrs. Ellen M. Pennell after some ten years service goes to the U. of O. for work in English with Miss Carson. Mrs. Pennell will also have charge of a ladies dormatory. Mr. L. A. Robinson will spend a year in Chicago University before returning to his work here. Miss Smith who has so long been connected with the T.

of the work. From all points of view this has been the most successful summer session ever held here and the teachers of the state have had opportunities not heretofore offered of getting the latest and best in all lines of methods and school management and supervision.

While a number of most excellent teachers have left the work here, a number have also been added. In A. L. Briggs, President of Drain, and in Mr. Fargo, of the Pendleton High school, the Oregon State Normal will gain some most valuable workers. These men have kept abreast with the best and are energetic, enthusiastic teachers. We bespeak for them the hearty cooperation and warm support of the entire Student body.

The coming session, which opens on the 14th, gives promise of being very successful both as to numbers and the inquiry is more and more from those who plan a definate course in teaching.

We believe that the real work of the Normal is rapidly felt and

A GOOD DAY FOR ACCIDENTS.

S. W. Doughty and I. Blodgett Severely Hurt.

LOCAL ITEMS OF MORE OR LESS IMPORT

Colonist Rates Are Now Effective From Eastern Points To Monmouth.

Tuesday morning about eight o'clock while S. W. Doughty and his brother were working on the residence of Frank Byers, between Monmouth and Independence, the scaffold fell and carried Mr. Doughty with it. In falling he struck the corner of the kitchen roof and bounded off falling in all about twenty feet. Two ribs were broken and his shoulder severely bruised, but the attending physician thinks that there are no internal injuries. He was brought home a short time after the accident and is getting along nicely. It is little short of a miracle that he was not killed by the fall as he weighs about 185 pounds.

Isaac Blodgett, of Blodgett's Valley, had a serious accident

This is a bird's eye view of the small village of Rickreall, sometimes called Dixie. It had many southern sympathizers during the Civil War. The town is located some ten miles from Salem in Polk County and the photo was taken at the turn of the century. The Rickreall can be seen flowing under the covered bridge; some of the old timers called this stream the La Creole. *(extreme lower right)*: Charles Bradford Whaley can be seen working in his potato patch. The barn to the right of the road was the town blacksmith shop owned by John Vaughn. Barn and house across the road belonged to Henry Clay followed by Peter Cook's General Store and the Community Church is beyond. *(left)*: Artisan Hall can be seen.

Derry Station in 1900 was the rail point serving the town of Rickreall in Polk County. This structure was built by the Western Oregon Railroad Company with living quarters for the agent and his family in the upstairs portion of the building. The small connecting building to the rear was used for storing baggage. It was added after the Southern Pacific became the owner of the line in 1879. The large woodpile to the rear was used for fuel for the woodburning locomotives. The wooden pen behind the station was for a cow and chickens. Those shown in the picture are *(left to right)*: Mira Lucas, Lynn Nesmith, Sarah E. Burch, small child with his mother is Kenneth Lucas and Kate Lucas. Benjamin Frank Lucas, not in the picture, was agent here for better than twenty-five years.

Eola was a small riverfront settlement a few miles west of Salem in Polk County. The one-room Eola School (photo taken in 1890) was erected in 1858 and for many years was recognized as the oldest operative public schoolhouse in the state. Today a new building has replaced the old structure. James J. Gwin, the first teacher, taught at a time when the school was only in session for three months of the year. His salary was paid by the students, starting at seven dollars then reduced to five dollars and finally settled at three dollars. In 1880, the county took over the payments. In those days, a teacher was chosen not for his scholarship so much as his physical strength. The boys were mature and husky and from the moment school opened in the winter until the closing in early spring, there was unrestrained hostility between the teacher and the pupils. This town lacked only a few votes of being selected as the state capitol back in the 1850s. One of the buildings was used by the Knights of the Golden Circle who met here during the Civil War to plot the downfall of the Union.

Eola was a flag stop on the Salem Falls City and Western Railway. (This means patrons must flag the train down by waving or some similar action so the engineer will understand that they want to board the train.) This open air station was one of many on this short twenty-seven mile railroad that operated between Salem and Black Rock and passed through cities of Dallas and Falls City.

SHERMAN COUNTY

This dry land farming scene shows a three section roller that scatters the planted seed. It is pulled by twenty-five draft animals. Ahead of the roller is a "grain drill" that opens, loosens, and plants the ground seed.

Grass Valley is ten miles south of Moro in Sherman County and located on the Shaniko branch of the Union Pacific Railroad. This town is an agricultural area showing Mid Columbia Elevator in the background which was used for storing large amounts of wheat before being shipped out by rail. The Union Pacific Railroad station is shown on the left. Photo was taken in 1945.

TILLAMOOK COUNTY

Citizens of Bay City in Tillamook County stand on the porches of their impressive new sixty thousand dollar hospital, a fifty room wooden structure built in 1909-10 by Dr. William Calvin Hawk. The site was selected because there was a common belief that the Bay City area had a great potential. It was located on a deep water shipping point on Tillamook Bay. Edward H. Harriman financially backed Elmer Lytle in building the Pacific Railway & Navigation Company by opening up rail service from Portland while James J. Hill had announced plans to make Bay City the terminus for the United Railways. The PRN was completed in 1911, but the electrified United Railways was never built.

This view of Bay City in Tillamook County looks south at the Southern Pacific railroad station in 1915. The city can be seen in the background. The trestle on the left is the walkway to the station while the trestle to the right is the rail spur serving the cannery.

Brighton Beach was a logging community on Nehalem Bay in Tillamook County. Shown here is a 1910 advertisement appearing in the *Pacific Monthly* offering lots for sale for $20.00. The Pacific Railway & Navigation Company (Southern Pacific) train left Portland at 7:20 AM and arrived in Brighton Beach at 1:21 PM, slightly longer than the ad reports.

The Brighton mill was owned by George and Thomas B. Watt, who started cutting lumber in 1912. This was one of the first mills to cut spruce timber used for airplane construction during World War I. In advertising for help wanted, their sign read "Married men with families will be given preference. No coolie labor will be employed. Saloons in the neighborhood are prohibited." Note the arrival of the daily passenger train enroute to Portland.

Some bathing beauties of the 1920s stroll along the sandy beach at Rockaway.

People waited patiently for the train at Rockaway in 1915. A corner of the railroad station can be seen *(left)* where Arthur R. "Art" Kirkham was the local ticket agent. The public will remember him as the chief radio and TV announcer at KOIN at Portland. Rockaway Creek is in the center of the photo with the beach and ocean in the background.

Cloverdale, Tillamook County, celebrates the Fourth of July with their own parade as Jess Kennedy drives his new 1913 Ford touring car over the town's unpaved street. Rachel Ward is the girl in the backseat with the long hair. The metal container on the running board is an acetylene gas generator. The base holds water and carbide pellets placed in the upper portion drop down into the water and produce the acetylene gas that operates the headlights. To the left can be seen the Cloverdale Cheese Factory with the town's hotel on the upper level. (Clyde Hudson photo)

Rollie Watson, editor of *The Tillamook Herald* (right), along with Henry Crenshaw (left) inspect their new 1905 A.O. Smith Flyer, a one cylinder two-seated gas engine with tiller steering.

UMATILLA COUNTY

An 1891 view of two structures in the old section of Umatilla in Umatilla County. Cherry's Saloon and Star Restaurant were both owned by A.M. Cherry, an ex-telegrapher. The rear of the saloon was a gambling area run by a corpulent old man named Jacques and as one newspaperman described him "as tough as a man in that position was supposed to be." Umatilla House for years was known only as "hotel" but apparently added the new title in reference to Umatilla House, the well-known hotel in The Dalles. It was run by an old trapper named Parker and his wife. Both structures were near the river's edge and faced the railroad station. The town in earlier days had been a terminus for the river boats on the upper Columbia River. Here they unloaded lading for a connection with the stages for inland points. Some of the important people residing in this town were: Lafayette Lane, a member of Congress; Zenas Ferry Moody, perhaps the earliest merchant in Umatilla who later became governor of Oregon from 1882–1886; Judge L.L. McArthur, member of the Oregon Supreme Court and later U.S. District Attorney in the Grover Cleveland administration.

Ukiah is in Umatilla county, some fifty miles south of Pendleton. Here is the main street in 1910. The buildings shown *(left to right)*: Frank Chamberlin's General Blacksmith shop with the word "garage" added to the sign later (a 1909 Huppmobile touring car can be seen in front); Ukiah Hotel and feed stable was operated by Despain Brothers; Ukiah Mercantile Company; Ukiah Creamery (white building) with Ward Emigh, owner. The Presbyterian church can be seen at the top of the hill. J.H. Wagner, a hardware and machinery dealer, is on the right.

UNION COUNTY

LaGrande is the county seat for Union County and is located on the western side of the Grande Ronde Valley in the Blue Mountains. Note the cast iron water trough taken in 1910 located in the middle of unpaved Adams Avenue. This nine foot tall "cast iron Mary," as it was called, was built in 1904 by the Women's Christian Temperance Union. It was demolished in 1924—yes! You guessed it—by a drunk driver who lost control of his automobile.

F.L. Meyers, cashier, can be seen at the extreme right of this inside view of the LaGrande National Bank. One of the tellers may have been Herman Clark, later a full professor at Willamette University at Salem. Note gas lights and coal-burning stove as seen in 1905.

Cove is in Union County. Shown is Main Street in 1912 during the First Annual Cherry Fair. Note group of wagons and buggies on hand to help celebrate. A 1912 Overland touring car can be seen. Some of the buildings shown *(left to right)*: Hotel Cove owned by Denham Wright; Leading Mercantile Company managed by C.J. Forsstrom. Buildings on the right side of the street include *(right to left)*: Stearns Fellbaum photo shop; Jos E. Tripper meat market; post office with Helen H. Ramsdell, postmaster; Cove State Bank with Jasper G. Stevens, President, and Hugh McCall as cashier. At the end of the block is an empty newspaper office. At one time this building housed *The Ledger*, published by J. Nat Hayden and later *The Courier*, edited by Willard N. Nelson.

Union, located in the extreme southeast corner of the Grande Ronde Valley in Union County, is often referred to as the "City of Victorian Heritage" because of its many beautiful homes. An early morning scene taken on Railroad Street in 1911 shows the Central Railroad of Oregon train pulled by locomotive #1, formerly O.R.N. 313, A 4-4-0 Rogers "yard goat." In the background can be seen the Union Flouring Mill who advertise their product "where snow white and gilt edge flour are made." Sign nailed to the pole in the front reads "no horses allowed to be tied to this pole."

WALLOWA COUNTY

Lostine is a small agricultural village situated on the south fork of the Wallowa River. It is served by Union Pacific Railroad off their Joseph Branch line. The daily passenger train stops to unload U.S. Mail, express, and passengers. Note stage on hand to meet the train.

A 1913 scene shows the Oregon Railway & Navigation Company passenger train stopping at Wallowa to detrain passengers. This town, platted in 1889 and incorporated in 1899, was named for the valley, the mountains, and the river.

Train Schedule: An 83 mile trip from LaGrande to Joseph:

LV LaGrande	10:00 AM Daily
AR Wallowa	12:55 PM
AR Joseph	2:00 PM

WASCO COUNTY

Great Southern Railway Train #1 in 1908 stops in front of the railroad station at Dufur in Wasco County. The train is pulled by a 2-6-0 oil-burning Baldwin locomotive with Engineer Albert Johnson at the controls. Conductor J.D. Tobin is standing on the ground helping passengers from the train. D. Spinning has backed his dray into position, ready to receive freight from the incoming train while the bus is ready to transport passengers to the Balch House, the town's leading hotel.

Antelope is in Wasco County and this scene shows the arrival of the stage in 1912 with the Antelope Hotel in the background. The daily stage makes the sixty mile run between Shaniko in Wasco County to Mitchell in Wheeler County, stopping at Antelope. The driver is believed to be John C. Todd. The Willamette Valley was settling down at this time, but central Oregon was still a western frontier. The town at that time was showing growth, but problems soon began to occur. The Columbia Southern Railway penetrated the area from Biggs on the Columbia River to Shaniko, a distance of seventy miles, but it was six miles short of reaching Antelope. The Oregon Trunk and the Des Chutes railroads built tracks down each side of the Deschutes Canyon to reach Bend. The new highway from The Dalles to California also missed the little town of Antelope. The town was forgotten except for the few old timers with their memories of a past life. More recently, a cult from India endeavored to take over the town, but at this writing, it too has failed.

WASHINGTON COUNTY

The annual horse fair for Washington County held in 1891. Looking east at Second & Main Streets in the town of Hillsboro are the following buildings *(left to right)*: Morgan Building built in 1890; the old Tualatin Hotel built in 1852 by Henry Wehrung. Hillsboro Commercial Bank is on the right. Note planked streets, boardwalk, and banners over the street for the celebration.

THE ARGUS.

VOL. 1.   HILLSBORO, OREGON, THURSDAY, JULY 26, 1894.   NO. 18.

TROOPS AT THE POLLS.

Unusual Sight Growing Out of the Strike.

UNION DELEGATES SUCCESSFUL.

STUNG TO THE QUICK.

Democratic Senators Smarting Under the Lash.

GROVER'S LETTER TO WILSON.

While Senators Have Been True to the Trusts, They Have Been False to Their Trust—Democratic Members of the Finance Committee Amazed.

FIGHT AT BLUEFIELDS.

A Coup d'Etat on the Part of the Indians.

DICTATOR LACAYO IS REMOVED.

NORTHWEST NEWS.

Washington.

WHAT M'DONALD SAYS

About Salmon Hatcheries in Oregon Streams.

IN REPLY TO SENATOR MITCHELL

This is a view of Beaverton in Washington County, showing Main Street in 1912. *(left to right)*: Mason P. Cady's Merchandise Store with a 1910 Maxwell touring car parked in front of the store; Bank of Beaverton with woodpile in the street to be used for heating the building; Beaverton bandstand used for the town's entertainment. On the opposite side of the street *(right to left)*: Della C. Fisher's front yard; Ray Morse Hall with dance floor upstairs; Lev Hardy confectionery; saloon owned by August Rossi and Joe Correri; Cady-Anderson Grocery Store. Note unpaved street and smoke from a steam locomotive as train is seen leaving the town.

In 1910, the small community of Buxton in Washington County, was primarily involved in farming and lumbering. Some of the town starting from the left side of the street *(left to right)*: Buxton Mercantile Company managed by Ralph Hannan and Elmer Pease; Buxton Hotel with Frank Donnell, proprietor; Post Office and building contractors office, both run by C.A. Peterson, Postmaster; Gregerson & Killburg's General Store; at the end of the block is Hannan & Christensen's shingle mill. Right side of the street: Buxton Box Factory with C.A. and Hans Peterson, owners. General store is run by J.H. Rinck.

Three car train of the Oregon Electric passes through Tonquin in Washington County and heads for Portland in 1912. Here is the schedule: OE Train #14 *The Rose City* leaves Salem 3:40 PM and arrives in Portland at 5:25 PM, with train passing through Tonquin at 4:20 PM.

OREGON ELECTRIC RAILWAY COMPANY

This Ticket will be sold by Conductors at Regular or Special Round Trip Rates to all Passengers boarding train at Non-Agency Stations, who request Round Trip Tickets. Conductors will punch Station, "FROM" and "TO," DATE and AMOUNT COLLECTED, and deliver Return Portion to Passenger. This Going Portion must be sent to Accounting Department with Train Reports. Punch "NOT GOOD AFTER" date.

Gen. Pass. Agt.

CONDUCTOR'S ROUND TRIP TICKET — GOING — FORM L57 — LANE-MILES STANDISH CO.

FROM TO: Portland, Jefferson St., Shops, Corbett St., View Point, Fulton Pk., Capitol Hill, Ryan Place, Multnomah, Shahapta, Maplewood, Garden Home, Firlock, Whitford, Beaverton, Medii, St. Mary's, Santa Rosa, Elmonica, Quatama, Orenco, Mineral, Sewell, Moffatt, Hillsboro, Oak Park, Pine Knot, Metzger, Greenburg, Tigard, Treco, Bonita, Durham, Golf, Tualatin, Nasoma, Tonquin, McLoy, Maiino, Wilsonville, Prahl, Butteville, Wallace, Donald, Fargo, Fellers, Broadacres, Logansnville, W. Woodburn, Scollard, Woodburn, St. Louis, Concomly, Waconda, Hopmere, Quinaby, Chemawa, Claxtar, Deaf School, Highland, Salem, Haselau, Croisan, Liversley, Finzer, Halls Ferry, E. Independ'ce, Orville, Loewt, Sidney, Wintel, Talbot, Dever, Conser, Albany, Pirtle, Gray, Corvallis, Verdure, Fayetteville, Pooler, Talma, Nixon, Carltner, Harrisburg, Junction City, Milorn, Meadow View, Awbrey, Enid, Ross, Avard

From — From Station not named write here and punch — **C** — To — For Destination

DATE ISSUED: Mar Feb Jan / Jun May Apr / Sep Aug July / Dec Nov Oct
3 2 1 / 6 5 4 / 9 8 7 / 12 11 10 / 15 14 13 / 18 17 16 / 21 20 19 / 24 23 22 / 27 26 25 / 30 29 28 / 31 X X / 1900 AND / 26 25 24 / 29 28 27

DOLLARS: 3 2 1 / 6 5 4 / 9 8 7
CENTS: 3 2 1 / 6 5 4 / 9 8 7 / 30 20 10 / 60 50 40 / 90 80 70

NOT GOOD AFTER: Mar Feb Jan / Jun May Apr / Sep Aug July / Dec Nov Oct
3 2 1 / 6 5 4 / 9 8 7 / 12 11 10 / 15 14 13 / 18 17 16 / 21 20 19 / 24 23 22 / 27 26 25 / 30 29 28 / 31 X X / 1900 AND / 26 25 24 / 29 28 27

IF GOOD FOR STOPOVER PUNCH HERE   HALF FARE ★

WHEELER COUNTY

Mitchell is located in the sagebrush and juniper of Bridge Creek Canyon in Wheeler County, one hundred and twenty miles southeast of The Dalles. Baily Butte is shown in the center of the picture. This photo was taken after the town had suffered a cloudburst in 1904, almost completely destroying it. William W. "Braudie" Johnson's blacksmith barn can be seen to the left. He served as the town's first postmaster. The Mitchell name has an interesting derivation, as told by one of the townspeople. A Mitchell wagon (brand name) was being driven from The Dalles to Canyon City carrying a full load of whiskey. The wagon broke down in the middle of nowhere. The driver, in a disgusted mood, sampled some of his lading. Soon, others passing by joined him. This was the starting of the Palace Saloon *(right)* and Mitchell was accepted as the name for the townsite.

Mitchell, Ore.

Mitchell was a semi-arid town as seen in the 1920s. It began its early existence by those raising cattle and horses, but with the increase in population, it became well-accepted as a farming and fruit growing area as well. The business section of the town, including saloons, occupied what might be called the lower level *(extreme right)* and was called "Tiger Town." The upper section was designated as "Piety Hill" *(left)* as it contained all of the churches and particularly the homes of the older citizens of Mitchell.

YAMHILL COUNTY

McMinnville in Yamhill County advertises itself as:

McMinnville is old enough to be substantial,
Young enough to be ambitious,
Big enough to be industrious, and
Small enough to be friendly.

Local farmers in 1902 brought in sacks of grain to be ground into flour by the Atlas Milling Company.

Southern Pacific's agricultural demonstration train rolled into McMinnville in 1908, pulled by SP-1395 a 4-4-0 Rogers locomotive. Skeptical but curious crowds visited the "University on Wheels" as it was called, and many of the farmers met with agricultural experts from Oregon Agricultural College (now called Oregon State University) to learn about new innovations to improve their livestock and crops. These lectures interested all types of farm people throughout the Willamette Valley as the train stopped at town after town.

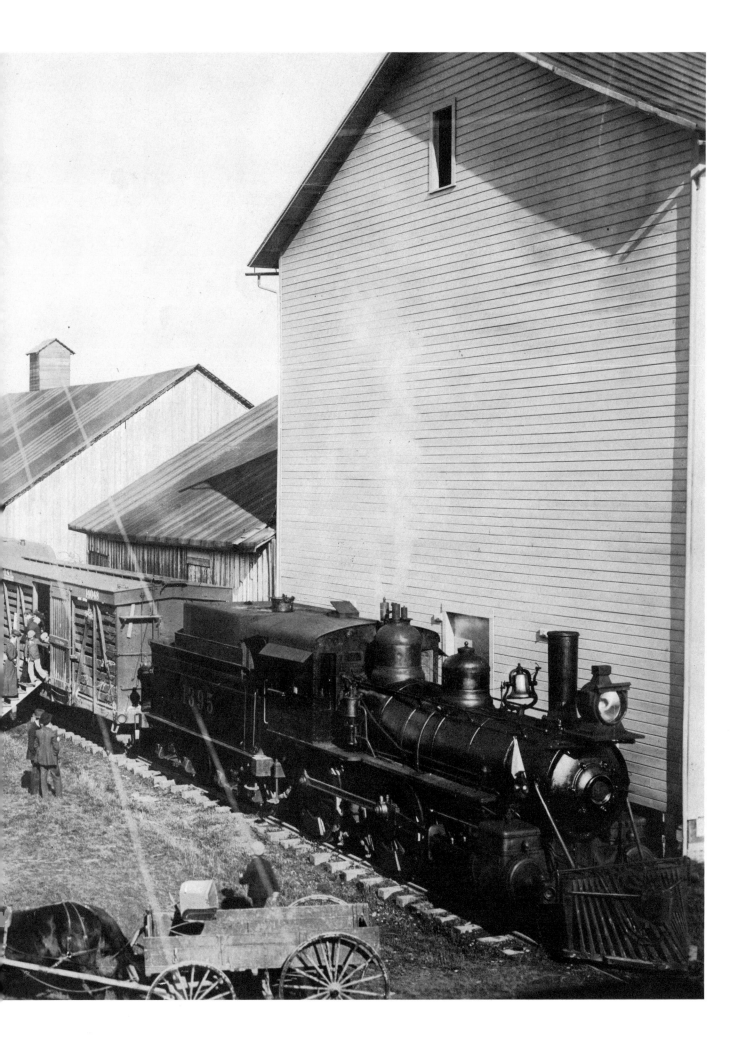

Yamhill County Reporter

VOL. XXXI. Entered at the Postoffice in McMinnville, as second-class matter. M'MINNVILLE, ORE., FRIDAY, NOV. 15, 1901. One Dollar if paid in advance, Single numbers five cents. NO. 48.

SAWYER'S EXCELSIOR
Keep Out the Wet
SAWYER'S
Excelsior Brand
OIL CLOTHING
The best waterproof garments in the world. Made from the best materials and warranted waterproof. Made to stand the roughest work and weather.
Look for the trade mark. If your dealer does not have them, write for catalogue to
S. Y. Kelling and Packing Co., Agts., San Francisco, or H. M. SAWYER & SON, Sole Mfrs., East Cambridge, Mass.

Wills' Modern Advertising Plan

Through the liberality of McMinnville's Leading Merchants,

A $100 A. B. Chase Parlor Organ

Purchased from the old reliable music dealer Geo. C. Will, Salem, Oregon, will be given to the one holding the largest number of coupons on November 16th, 1901. All coupons must be signed by the merchant issuing the coupon, and by the holder of same. The purchaser can give his or her coupons to some one else and let them sign them. It will pay you to trade at the following stores and receive a coupon with every 25c CASH purchase:

McMinnville Grange & Farmers store, Dry Goods, Clothing & Shoes. Organ on exhibition at this store.
H. C. Burns, Furniture Store.
J. G. Wiesner—Cigars and Tobacco.
Wm. F. Dielschneider & Bro., jewelers.
Willard & Ehrman & Co., meat market.
Rogers Bros., Drugstore.
T. A. White—White's Restaurant.
S. P. Houser—Second hand store and Sewing Machines.
Geo. L. Williams—Bookstore.
F. W. Spencer—Hardware, Farm Machinery, Bicycles and Sewing Machines.
J. S. Roscoe—Bicycle Sundries and Repairs.
A. J. Lolan, Harness Shop.
Triplett & Hendershott—Confectionery
C. F. Daniels—Feed, Seed & Produce.
Lambert Bros.—Groceries & Commission.

TAKE A WALK.

The dwellers in the arctic regions view the midnight sun without emotion; Niagara has no interest or charm to those who have passed their lives within sound of its dashing, and even its thunders are not audible to them. It is a very common old saying that familiarity breeds contempt, and it also may be said that the continued contemplation of our surroundings will result in making most beautiful objects commonplace. Those who do not live within the zone of these two wonders will journey across seas and continents to behold their grandeur, and stand amazed at the magnificence of the one and the physical splendor of the other. But to bring the matter home, how few of us realize the quiet beauty that can be enjoyed by a survey of the environments of our own little city. Take a walk. Shake off the misty cobwebs and look beyond brick walls. Get out from the narrow channels of business. Stop figuring interest long enough to allow yourself to commingle for an hour with outdoor thoughts, where your soul will have a chance to broaden with a vision and an inspiration that reaches beyond the city limits—and that must do so if this, the fairest city in the valley, is to reach out and build up on the business material within reach of her.

Go, climb one of the hills to the west, and then turn and look at the valley as it stretches away till it ends in a hazy mist in the direction of the eternal snows on the crest of Hood and Jefferson, the grand sentinels that stand guard over the garden spot of earth. That row of gold and crimson that winds in and out of the dark green of cedar and fir marks the sinuous course of the Yamhill, its banks bordered with vegetation newly painted by the frost artist, and its bosom assisting to carry to the markets of the world our too meager commerce.

The old town with its cozy homes and its tall steeples nestles securely in the honor and virtue of its past history. Now and then a puff of smoke from a chimney tells that the city is not destitute of industry. But mark, while you gaze, the progressive city of which you

TWO RECEPTIONS.

Many Friends Honor the Hoberg Anniversary.

The Methodist church was comfortably filled Tuesday evening with friends of Rev. and Mrs. Joseph Hoberg, for the purpose of uniting in a public celebration of their 50th wedding anniversary. That chief embodiment of wit, Rev. H. T. Atkinson, presided in a most efficient manner. The various sons-in-law and grandchildren occupied front seats, while the parents and their four sons and four daughters occupied the platform. The program opened with a good old Methodist hymn, followed by invocation by Rev. L. W. Riley of the Baptist church. Rev. Platt of the Christian church read the 71st Psalm. B. F. Rhodes was announced as the first speaker, but was unavoidably kept away. President Boardman came next. He did not feel that one of his age and experience could measure up to the demands of the occasion, but he congratulated the aged people on their anniversary, and the graceful manner in which they are growing old. His earliest recollection of a preacher was Father Hoberg, whose personality had stamped an indelible influence for good upon him. He thought growing old gracefully was almost a lost art, and he coveted no diviner blessing than that it might be his privilege to thus grow old.

Prof. W. A. Pettis of Salem was present and favored the audience with the violin variations of "Home, Sweet Home," in an artistic manner.

Rev. A. J. Hunsaker addressed the meeting briefly, and said his first meeting with Bro Hoberg was 25 years ago at a place where the latter was seeking a drink—of water. He spoke of the ultra-Baptist character of the program, and emphasized the beauty and advantages of smiling countenances, such as the subjects of the meeting had always displayed.

C. P. Nelson gave some early recollections of Father Hoberg, covering a period of 20 years in Sunday school work, and closed with an expression of good wishes. The "Olive Branches," (children) sang "Home, Sweet Home," and to satisfy a demand for more, gave "Hear 'Dem Bells." All have good voices, and enjoy singing.

To all these tributes Father Hoberg gave splendid response, although claiming that the "wind had been taken out of his sails." As is characteristic, he attributed all joys and successes of life as coming from God, in whom they had always maintained an unfaltering trust. Mother Hoberg, as usual, had to quietly sit under the fire of several good-natured thrusts from her spouse, and Brother Hunsaker came in for his share also.

DEATH OF WILLIAM D. WRIGHT.

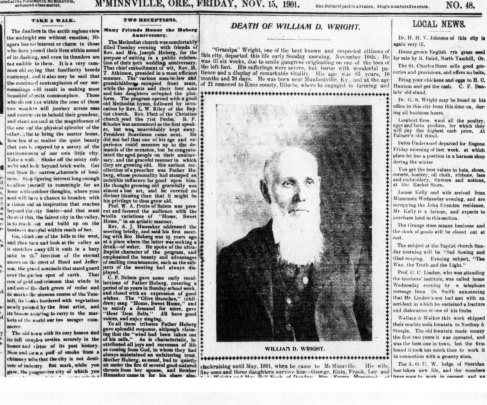

"Grandpa" Wright, one of the best known and respected citizens of this city, departed this life early Sunday morning, November 10th. He was ill six weeks, due to senile gangrene originating on one of the toes of the left foot. His sufferings were severe, but borne with wonderful patience and a display of remarkable vitality. His age was 83 years, 10 months and 28 days. He was born near Munfordville, Ky., and at the age of 21 removed to Knox county, Illinois, where he engaged in farming and

WILLIAM D. WRIGHT.

stockraising until May, 1881, when he came to McMinnville. His wife, five sons and three daughters survive him—George, Elsia, Frank, Lee and

LOCAL NEWS.

Dr. H. H. V. Johnson of this city is again very ill.

Home grown English rye grass seed for sale by R. Baird, North Yamhill, Or.

The St. Charles Store sells good groceries and provisions, and offers no baits.

Bring your chickens and eggs to H. C. Hannon and get the cash. C. F. Daniels' old stand.

Dr. G. S. Wright may be found in his office in this city from this time on, during all business hours.

Lambert Bros. want all the poultry, eggs and farm produce, for which they will pay the highest cash price. At Palmer's old stand.

Delos Underwood departed for Eugene Friday morning of last week, at which place he has a position in a harness shop during the winter.

You get the best values in hats, shoes, corsets, hosiery, oil cloth, ribbons, lace and embroidery, tinware and notions, at the Racket Store.

James Kelly and wife arrived from Minnesota Wednesday evening, and are occupying the John Evenden residence. Mr. Kelly is a farmer, and expects to purchase land in this section.

The Grange store means business and the stock of goods will be closed out at cost.

The subject at the Baptist church Sunday morning will be "Sad Sowing and Glad reaping. Evening subject, "The Way, the Truth and the Light."

Prof. C. C. Linden, who was attending the teachers' institute, was called home Wednesday evening by a telephone message from Dr. Smith announcing that Mr. Linden's son had met with an accident in which he sustained a fracture and dislocation of one of his limbs.

Wallace & Walker this week shipped their marble soda fountain to Northup & Sturgis. The old fountain made money the first two years it was operated, and was the best one in town, but the firm found it took too much time to work it in connection with a grocery store.

The A. O. U. W. lodge of Sheridan has taken new life, and the members have gone to work in earnest, and we

THE NEWS-REPORTER

VOLUME 75 THE NEWS-REPORTER, McMINNVILLE, OREGON THURSDAY, MAY 29, 1947 NUMBER 28

Linfield Plans Two Services Sunday, June 1

Outstanding Speakers To Bring Messages

The Linfield college baccalaureate service will take place Sunday morning, June 1 at 11:00 a. m. at the First Baptist church with Dean Cyril F. Richards of Denison University, Granville, Ohio, delivering the message. Dean Richards is a member of the class of 1918.

Dean Richards' topic will be "One World—One Mind".

The commencement services will take place the same day at 4:00 p. m. also at the First Baptist church. The speaker will be Benjamin H. Kizer, who is one of the outstanding leaders of the northwest and recognized internationally for his progressive idealism and administrative abilities. He was called from his active practice of law in the city of Spokane in 1944 to become the director of UNRRA in China. He served there from 1944 until the UNRRA was dissolved in 1946.

Mr. Kizer was a student of Mrs. F. E. R. Linfield and will speak on the subject: "China Confronts Western Civilization."

Cub Scout Pack To Have Picnic At City Park

Monday, June 2, the McMinnville Cub Scout Pack will meet at the city park at 6 p. m. for a potluck picnic. It is important that the entire family be present to take part. Each Den Mother will make arrangements with the den families for food.

The program, as outlined by Cubmaster Ernest Brown, will include competitive games for which appropriate prizes, furnished by representative city merchants, will be awarded. The den chiefs who have completed a successful year's program will have special recognition. Those boys graduated into Boy Scouts will be given a Webelos ceremony.

This is the final regular meeting of the year, according to Rex Warren, chairman of the sponsoring committee, and all den families are urged to take part.

Uni. of Oregon to Hold Reunion Weekend

Many From Here Will Attend Youth For Christ

Buses will leave at 5:00 p. m. Friday from the First Baptist church for Portland bringing many people from here to Multnomah Stadium where the Portland Youth for Christ is staging a big rally. People from all over the Northwest will be present to hear Rev. Charles E. Fuller, of The Old Fashioned Revival Hour radio program, Rudy Atwood, piano player, Old Fashioned Revival Hour Quartet, Cliff Barrows who will be song leader, a 500 voice choir and Torrey Johnson, who just returned from a Youth for Christ team tour of Europe and especially Germany. Cliff Barrows, also, just returned from a trip to England and parts of Europe and was at the McMinnville rally a couple of weeks ago.

The stadium has been marked off and McMinnville Youth for Christ section is No. 10, through gate 10.

Those going on the buses should bring their lunch. Drinks will be furnished on the buses.

4-H'ers To Get Merit Awards For Improving Job Methods On Farms

4-H Club members in Oregon again have an opportunity this year to win special recognition for developing methods that will simplify their farm and home jobs. Recognition in the form of merit awards will be given on county, state and national levels in the 4-H Better Methods Electric Activity, the National Committee on Boys and Girls Club Work has announced.

Members need not have electricity on their farms to take part in this activity, which may be applied to all types of 4-H Club work.

Last year county Winners were named in Douglis, Marion and Yamhill counties. Each county winner receives a gold-filled medal of honor.

High School

Vets Purchase Homes, Farms And Businesses

8000 Veterans Have Loans Totaling $37,538,000

Nearly 8,000 Oregon veterans have realized wartime dreams of a home, farm or small business of their own with the aid of G. I. loans amounting to $37,538,000, H. K. Clark, Veterans' Administration contact representative here, announced.

The VA's regional office in Portland has informed Clark that, up to May 1, approvals have been granted for G. I. loans on 6,304 homes, 1,155 small businesses and 456 farms. These loans, made to veterans by private lending institutions and backed by VA guaranty, averaged $5,054 on homes, $3,300 on businesses and $4,000 on farms.

Actual guarantees under the G. I. bill have averaged 47 per cent of each loan. Only a small percentage of loans have been large enough to use the maximum guaranty of $4,000 on real property or $2,000 on non-real business property; the guaranteed portion cannot be more than half the entire loan.

Since the start of this year, the VA has approved 1,916 loans for guaranty in Oregon, totaling $9,711,650. Reflecting a general slow-up on realty sales, veterans' applications have slipped from a high of 130 a week in April to slightly fewer than 100 a week in May, Clark revealed.

"Veterans are less willing now to pay exorbitant prices for homes, and many are less able to because of higher living costs and consequent depletion of savings," the VA aide explained. "On the slackening market now, property sellers seem more willing to reduce their prices to meet the VA's anti-inflationary appraisals."

Dr. A. L. Groom Elected President of Dental Assn.

10 Yamhill Students Will Receive Degrees At Oregon State College

McMinnville, Carlton and Dundee will be represented by 10 students among 924 seniors and graduate students to receive degrees at Oregon State college at the seventy-eighth annual commencement Sunday, June eighth.

This will be the largest graduating class in the history of the college, the previous record number being 790 in 1940.

Helen Jean Taylor of McMinnville and Betty Ann Meyer and Florence Hubbard Uhlig of Dundee are among 107 seniors being graduated in home economics; Ernest Frank Jernstedt and Shirley Ann Noble of McMinnville and Frederick Gordon Meyer of Dundee will receive degrees in agriculture; Mary Lois Glentzer and Joan Mead Merritt of McMinnvill are among 90 getting degrees in the school of science; Edna Luciele Rytting of McMinnville is completing the course in business and industry; and Arthur Ray Williams of Carlton will be graduated in engineering.

Oregon Nut Growers Select Board Officers

Lloyd C. Baron was named new manager of Oregon Nut Growers, Inc., by the board of directors at a meeting on Tuesday. His appointment becomes effective June 1. He succeeds John E. Trunk, who becomes general manager of Northwest Nut Growers on June 1.

At a directors' meeting held on May 10 the following directors of Oregon Nut Growers, Inc., were named to serve on the Northwest Nut Growers' board: President W. J. Sullivan of Newberg, John C. Dixon of Dundee and George Repp of Sherwood and Portland.

Queen To Be Chosen For St. Paul Rodeo

It's queen selection time for the

Memorial Day Programs To Be At Cemeteries

Memorial Day in McMinnville will be observed without a parade this year. Stores and banks will be closed but special services at the cemeteries by various veterans' organizations will be the order of the day. Graveside services will be under the direction of the American Legion and the Veterans of Foreign Wars.

Veterans will gather at the armory at 10:00 a. m. and go in a body to the Masonic, Evergreen and Catholic cemeteries respectively.

4-H Sewing Clubs Hold Style Revue

The 4-H sewing clubs from the McMinnville, Dayton, Sheridan, Carlton area held their style revue Friday, May 23 in the Methodist church in McMinnville. Miss Helen Cowgill, assistant state 4-H club leader, acted as judge of the dresses and aprons. Scholarships were awarded to Sherry Jack of Carlton; Marion Maynard of McMinnville; Joan Bride of McMinnville, Jane Bernards of McMinnville and Janet Lyons of Dayton. These Scholarships are for the summer school held each year at Oregon State college for outstanding 4-H club members.

A pie auction was held after the revue, the proceeds to be used by the leaders' association to further club work. Refreshments were served by Mrs. H. C. Maynard and Mrs. William M. Perry.

Mother of Prominent Oregon Authors Dies

Mrs. Jane Ann Hammond Case, 82, mother of two Oregon authors, died May 24 after a stroke suffered five weeks ago. Her eight children included Robert Ormond Case, Portland,

Edgar Meresse Called By Death

News-Reporter Publisher Passes Away

Edgar Meresse, 69, publisher of The News-Reporter for the past 37 years died Friday at the McMinnville hospital following seven weeks of illness.

Mr. Meresse came to McMinnville in 1910 and purchased The News-Reporter in partnership with Ren Rosensteel.

He was born in France in 1877 coming to this country with his parents at the age of ten, settling in Oregon City and attended public schools. He attended Pacific University and graduated from Willamette University where he edited the first Willamette year book.

Prior to coming to McMinnville he did reporting on newspapers at Forest Grove, The Dalles and Salem.

He was married to Mabel Bryant at Portland in 1915, who survives him. A brother, Able Meresse, a publisher at White Salmon, Wash., also survives.

Mr. Meresse was a member of the McMinnville Elks lodge and a charter member of the Rotary club.

Funeral services were held Monday at 2 p. m. at Macy & Sons chapel. The service was conducted by Rev. C. C. Barnes of the Presbyterian church. Final rites were held at Forest View cemetery at Forest Grove.

Pallbearers were Stanley Cellers, George Neuner, Frank Wortman, Dr. B. F. Whitmer, Ed Peterson and Lyle Briedwell.

In the passing of our editor The News-Reporter staff feel we have lost a kind and sincere friend and we will always cherish the memory of him. We feel that his passing is a deep loss not only to us but to the entire community he loved and served so ably. He became interested in journalism in his school days and his work was a joy to him as he followed it through the years. We sympathize with his many friends in his passing.

Carpenters Are Needed For Work on Guam

Footloose carpenters between the ages of 21 and 50 wanting to build a nest egg by saving six out of seven paychecks are being recruited by the Oregon State Employment Service for work on Guam, officials announced, adding that a minimum of 400 men are needed at once.

Springbrook is in Yamhill County eighteen miles northeast of McMinnville. A Southern Pacific steam passenger train in 1905 stops in front of the open-air railroad station *(center)*. The store *(left)* facing Gibbs Road was built by Benjamin F. Halladay in 1896. The town, originally called Hoskins, applied for a post office, but found the name was already in use in Benton County. Cyrus E. Hoskins, whose farm can be seen to the far right, called his home Springbrook. It was decided to use this name for the town.

Flora Logging Company has scalped all of the closeby timber and is now moving camp and all to a new location.

33% of all Oregon trees are Douglas Fir.
59% of all forest products manufactured in Oregon are from Douglas Fir.

GIFFORD PHOTOS

Benjamin Arthur Gifford
"The Dean of Oregon Photographers"
Born: Danby, Illinois
August 11, 1859
Died: Vancouver, Washington
March 5, 1936

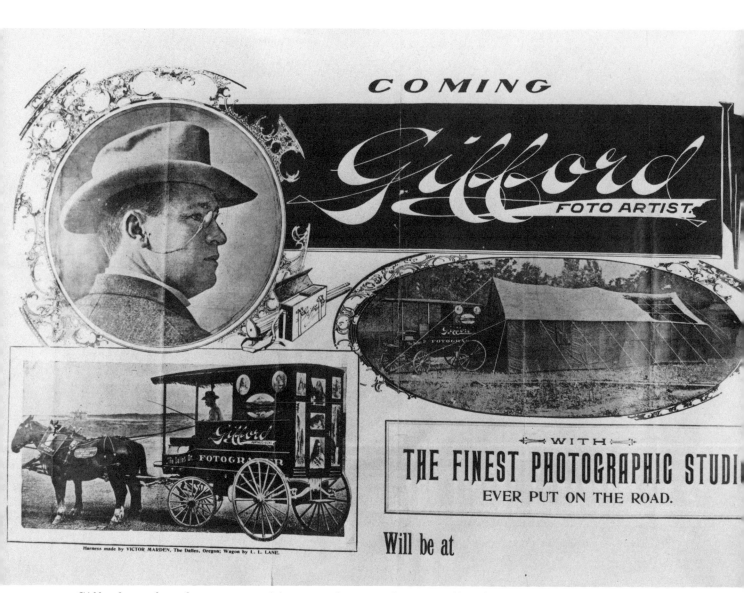

Gifford was best-known as an itinerant photographer traveling from town to town. One of his display posters used at the turn of the century was often shown before Mr. Gifford and his associates arrived. Note the opening in the roof of the tent *(center-right)*, allowing natural light to enter. This light was necessary for taking portrait photos.

A little relaxation is probably taken somewhere in Morrow County for Mr. and Mrs. Gifford and his assistant, Charles Y. Lamb and wife. Mr. Gifford's son, Ralph Irving Gifford (1894–1947) is the small nine-year-old boy shown. He followed his father's profession and became the first photographer for the Oregon State Highway Commission.

The Dalles is the county seat of Wasco County. A scene taken in 1903 shows the wood scow *Reliance* on Mill Creek *(center)* loaded with a cargo of wood. Owners of these flat-bottom barges with only wind and sail for motive power cut wood along the banks of the Columbia River and transported it to The Dalles for heating and industrial purposes. Note mast on the barges. *The Western Queen*, wood-burning side wheeler, *(center)* was the ferry used for service across the Columbia River to the Washington side of the river. Boat house *(right)* was owned by Dalles Portland & Astoria Navigation Company, owners of steamboats running on the Columbia River.

Fort Dalles bakery was one of two buildings left standing after the fort was destroyed in 1868. The 1908 photo shows the poet, Joaquin Miller, visiting with Fred Benzer, the old fort baker who stayed on after the fire selling bread to the people of The Dalles in Wasco County.

Joseph Luxello, Yakima Indian Chief taken in 1900, is shown seated in the chair-like section of Pulpit Rock, a natural basaltic pillar now used for Easter services and a sight-seeing point at The Dalles. He is seen imitating Jason Lee, the famous Methodist minister. Luxello returned to The Dalles frequently as it was here he was baptized in 1840 into the Christian faith.

This scene was taken in the dalles of the narrows of the Columbia River at The Dalles in Wasco County. This area is now entirely submerged by The Dalles Dam reservoir. Note the fish wheels in the background. Mr. Gifford often used some of his own family and photo assistants to be a part of the picture as he has done here.

In 1913-14, Mr. Gifford took this photo near Multnomah Falls looking east during the construction of the Columbia River Highway. Union Pacific tracks can be seen in the center of the picture.

Ione is in Morrow County; this photo was taken in 1903. The town is located on a level tract of land in Willow Creek Valley, some thirty miles from the Columbia River. The two buildings shown *(front)* are the Farmers Warehouse and Kerr Gifford & Company (Union Pacific). The two story wooden school building *(left)* can be seen at the foot of the hill. A temporary tent *(left & front)* was used by Mr. Gifford as a portrait studio and finishing laboratory as they covered the various towns.

Matthew "Scotty" Thorburn is shown with his two faithful and ever-watchful dogs as they overlook the flock of sheep near Kingsley some twenty-three miles south of The Dalles in Wasco County. This 1900 photo was labeled "Shepherd of the Hills," a title taken from one of Harold Bell Wright's best-selling novels.

A band of sheep are moved by barge across the Columbia River near Maryhill, then called Columbus, to the closest rail point, then on the Oregon side of the river.

"Schan-na-wick," translated "sharp eyes" was chief of the Wascoes for over half a century. His corpulence prohibited him from active participation with his people. Photo was taken in 1905 when "sharp eyes" was at the age of seventy-two. One of the exciting events in old "sharp eyes" career was an attempt he made to help the white people locate Captain Jack, the notorious and sought-after leader of the murderous Modoc Indians, who killed General Edward R.S. Canby at a peace parley in Southern Oregon. He found the troublesome Indian and fired upon him, but the bullet went wild and inadvertently killed Captain Jack's mother. The Modocs were aroused and it became necessary for "sharp eyes" to vacate the area as fast as possible.

GIFFORD 230 MT. HOOD FROM LOST LAKE. HEIGHT 11,225 FEET

Mount Hood from Lost Lake, a sunrise scene taken before the turn of the century. This is considered the finest black and white photograph ever made of this mountain. It remains a classic today, despite the vast improvement in cameras and film. Before this picture began to circulate across the nation, only a handful of adventurous men had glimpsed this exultant view. Getting to Lost Lake high in the mountainous southwesterly corner of Hood River County proved an accomplishment in itself. Mr. Gifford was offered one thousand dollars for the negative, but refused the offer. Seeing Lost Lake and Mount Hood became a goal for thousands of people. Many who came to the Hood River Valley during the heavy growth of the early 1900s admitted the beautiful picture encouraged their coming.

234 NORTH ABUTMENT TO BRIDGE OF THE GODS AND CASCADES OF THE COLUMBIA

"North Abutment to Bridge of the Gods" was the caption Mr. Gifford gave to this picture taken in 1900 from the Oregon side of the Columbia River looking towards the Washington side. Table Mountain *(center)* covered with snow is the highest peak shown; below this peak are layers of sedimentary rock. Hundreds of years ago, a landslide of this material is believed to have dammed the river at this point. The barrier may have resulted in a causeway across the river much like what was related in the Indian legend told by Frederic Homer Balch in *The Bridge of the Gods*. Along the shoreline are shown numerous fishwheels, most of them belonging to the Frank Manley Warren Packing Company. Fishwheel #16 "the big wheel" *(left)* was constructed by a hardy band of Swedish people who learned this type of work in the old country. In 1926, the voters of Oregon outlawed the use of all fishwheels. In the center of the picture, a small section of the trackage of the old Cascade Portage Railroad can be seen.

This photo was taken July 20, 1905, as the sun was setting on the Columbia River and shadows began to gather over the hills. The Indians, after seeing the photo, called it "Wa-Ne-Ka" ("Halo of the Evening Sun"). Mr. Gifford believes "it was the most artistic and harmonious mantel picture ever produced." This scene was taken about twenty-three miles east of The Dalles. He endeavored to photograph the Indians living in their tepees. With the usual perversity and superstitions of their race, they declined to have their picture taken. The only living thing left for Mr. Gifford to photograph was an Indian dog on guard outside the larger tepee.

This picture was taken on July 20, 1905. Mr. Gifford explains that it was made under rather peculiar circumstances:

As I turned my back on the tepees to take the cap off my camera, a rock struck close to me. I turned quickly, but couldn't see anyone. Once more, I turned my back and a rock whizzed by my head. This time I ran toward one of the tepees. Several Indians were hiding behind. They declined to have their picture taken, only one ill-favored squaw did allow a photo to be made.

Indians are shown spearing salmon at Celilo on the Columbia River. They have preserved for us their ancient use of the wooden spear, the kind used before the coming of the white man.

Mr. Gifford lived in The Dalles from 1898 to 1910. During this time, he became very interested in the Columbia River Indians and made many photographs portraying their lifestyle.

Loading a pine log around the turn of the century onto a flat bed wagon. Two heavy beams lodged firmly into the ground are used as trackage. The heavy log is being rolled by a dead center chain: one end is fastened to the deck of the rig while the other end is pulled by a set of horses not shown in the picture. Note "log bunks" on the right side of the rig to prevent the log from rolling off of the wagon.

OREGON HUMOR

A TRANSFORMATION.

From the *West Shore Magazine* published in Portland from 1875 to 1891.

GREETINGS

*We came here for a change and rest.
The Waiter gets the change and
the Hotel gets the Rest.*

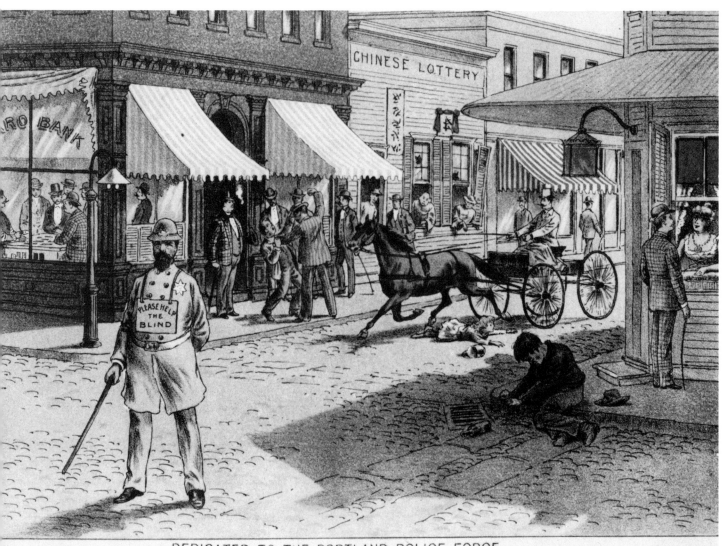

DEDICATED TO THE PORTLAND POLICE FORCE.

From *West Shore Magazine*

Oregon apples from Hood River in Hood River County.

Oregon pears from Medford in Jackson County.

Oregon watermelons from Hermiston in Umatilla County.

Oregon blackberries from Newberg in Yamhill County.

Oregon women were given the
vote in November, 1912.

A lady there was who said "Why
Should men have the vote and not I?
    To call this democracy,
    Is naught but hypocrisy,—
I'll get me the ballot or die!"